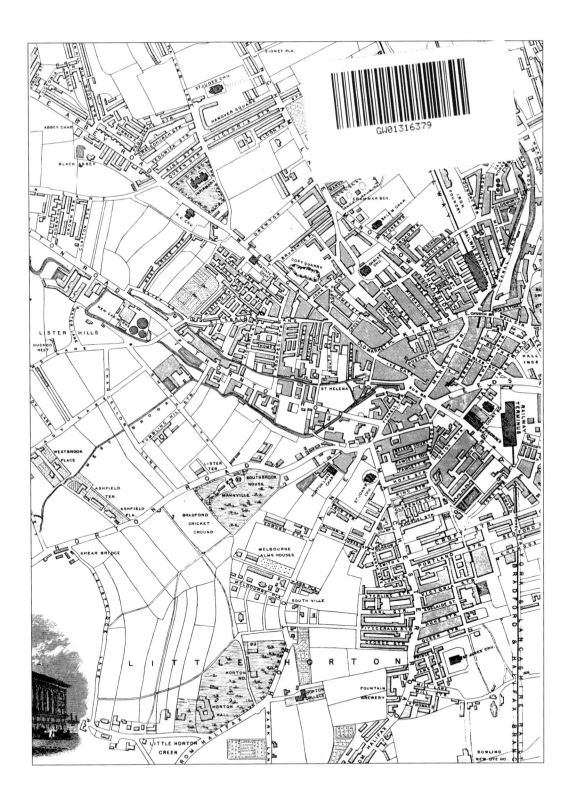

Bradford. Mid 19th Century. Horton Hall bottom left.

Published in 2000 by
Bradford Libraries

© Astrid Hansen 2000

All rights reserved.
Without limiting the rights under copyright
reserved above, no part of this publication may be
reproduced, stored in or introduced into a retrieval system,
or transmitted, in any form or by any means (electronic, mechanical,
photocopying, recording or otherwise) without the prior
written permission of both the copyright owner and
the above publisher of this book.

Printed by The Amadeus Press, Cleckheaton, Bradford
Graphic Layout by Highlight Type Bureau Ltd, Bradford
Cover Design by Phil Hansen

ISBN 0-907734-58-8

SHARP TO BLUNT

THE STORY OF
HORTON HALL, BRADFORD
AND SOME OF ITS OCCUPANTS

by

Astrid Hansen

© 2000

Contents

Chapter 1	Sharp	9
Chapter 2	Christophers, Jameses, Johns and Thomases	15
Chapter 3	Sharps at War	18
Chapter 4	Prosperity	22
Chapter 5	"The Incomparable Mr. Sharp"	30
Chapter 6	A Gentleman's Residence	43
Chapter 7	John Wood and the Ten Hours Bill	46
Chapter 8	Samuel Hailstone and William Sharp	50
Chapter 9	The Biggest Hailstone	54
Chapter 10	For Sale	61
Chapter 11	Not Quite a Palace	68
Chapter 12	Blunt	74
Chapter 13	Epilogue	82

Introduction

While writing the history of Bradford Diocese, I realised that Bishop Blunt was the last person to live in the house that had been built by the Sharps. Here, I felt, was a title waiting for a book!

I remember the existence of this lovely old house, and often wondered about its history and how it had been allowed to come to such a sorry end.

The more I looked into the families associated with Horton Hall, the more I discovered stories that deserve to be told and Bradfordians of whom there is good reason to be proud. The Sharps were an amazing family, and some of those who subsequently lived in their home made their own contributions to local and national history. Not least among these contributions is the encounter leading to the Ten Hours Bill. This was the beginning of the end of the shameful and inhuman treatment of factory workers which so marred the Industrial Revolution throughout the nation.

I have covered a span of approximately 750 years of social history through the fortunes of the occupants of one house.

It is a complicated story, particularly in the early years, and I soon found contradictions in some of the existing accounts, and confusions of generations and family trees. Some of these have persisted into beliefs expressed in more recent comments. Therefore I have set out to provide an accurate account, verifying as much as possible from a variety of sources. I apologise in advance for the errors which readers of history almost inevitably find!

As well as quoting from Bradford's 19th century historians, I have turned to the Sharp Powell archives, the Hailstone papers in York, Bradford Council Records, members of the Blunt and Hailstone families, and contemporary writers on the history of astronomy.

I am most grateful to the following for help and encouragement:
Mr. and Mrs. David Blunt, Mr. Alan Hitchcock, Mr. John Hitchcock, Mr. Howard Miller, Dr. Allan Chapman, Dr. Anita McConnell (New Dictionary of National Biography), Mr. Rusty MacLean (Librarian and Archivist, Rugby School), Sir Ernest Hall, Mr. George Sheeran, Mr. John Ayers, Mr Bob Duckett and staff of Bradford Library Local Studies Department, Bradford District Archives, York Museums, National Monuments Record Office, the Royal Astronomical Society, the Science Museum London, the National Maritime Museum.

AGH

Chapter 1
Sharp

"Pity poor Bradford", wailed the ghost of Bolling Hall, reputedly causing the Royalist Commander, the Earl of Newcastle, to deal mercifully with the population when his forces claimed the town in 1643.

Where were you, ghost, when you should have been wailing in the ears of developers and planners in our own time?

Bradford historian William Cudworth, writing in 1889, referred to Horton Hall as "a fair specimen of an Elizabethan residence of one of the smaller gentry, such indeed as abound in the neighbourhood of Bradford."

Where are they now? A handful remain in varying states of preservation, modification and disguise, but so many are gone. The Manor Hall, which once graced Kirkgate, its gardens and orchards stretching back to the present John Street, is long gone; the Halls of Bierley, Allerton, Heaton and Manningham, Stott Hill House, Shuttleworth Hall, Miryshay and others, all demolished. And Horton Hall is gone, one of the oldest, loveliest, strangest; home over the centuries to many significant characters in Bradford's story.

The exact age of the earliest part of Horton Hall is not known, but William Cudworth, in his "Life and Correspondence of Abraham Sharp", published in 1889 refers to "Abraham Sharp born at Little Horton in 1653, his family having resided in the same district for over 500 years before him," which locates Sharps in Horton in the middle of the 12th century, in an England just emerging from the long and chaotic power struggle between rival claimants to the English crown, Stephen and Matilda. This was a hard and dangerous feudal world. In it the Sharps not only survived, but succeeded, rising, we cannot know how, to the point at which the Lord of the Manor, William de Leventhorpe, in 1365 conveyed to Thomas Sharp two bovates or oxgangs, and a messuage in Little Horton, adjoining lands belonging to the Abbot of Kirkstall. A bovate is the area of land an ox could plough in a season, approximately thirteen acres. Twenty six acres and a house was an appreciable holding.

In 1390 a further half acre of land was granted by William, son of John de Bradford, to John, son of Thomas Sharp. In the same year, William de Leventhorpe granted the Manor of Leventhorpe in Bradforddale to members of the Sharp and de Horton families, but in 1402 Thomas, son of John Sharp of Little Horton, released his rights in the manor to William de Leventhorpe's son Geoffrey.

The names of a John Sharp and his son Christopher appear on a deed during the reign of King Edward IV (1461-1483).

Clement Richardson in his "Geography of Bradford" (University of Bradford 1976) says that the earliest written references to Great and Little Horton do not appear until the period 1100 - 1200 AD. but place names with the element "tun" or "ton", meaning farmstead, are generally held to date from the Old English period from the 5th to 11th century. A meaning he suggests for Horton is "filthy farm", which might well have applied to an early hovel on inhospitable ground. John James however quotes Dr.T.D. Whitaker, in his celebrated "History of Craven", referring to Horton in Ribblesdale, as possibly derived from Horetown, an area often "gray with sleet when the lower grounds are unsprinkled." Whether dirty or cold, or both, there is no doubt farms in the Horton area of Bradford would have been struggling and have needed a good acreage to support a family. Richardson demonstrates from the geology of Bradford Dale how poor the soil would have been in many parts. Settlements mentioned in the Domesday survey were spaced at one and a half to two miles apart, reflecting, he suggests, "the agricultural spatial threshold required to support farm populations operating a system of cereal cultivation with fallowing every second or third year." Some cereal crops were necessary, even though the ground might be scarcely suitable, since these early settlements needed to be self sufficient.

To make matters worse, the harrying of the north in 1070 had left much of the dale depopulated and waste. Land values in Yorkshire fell by as much as two thirds during this time.

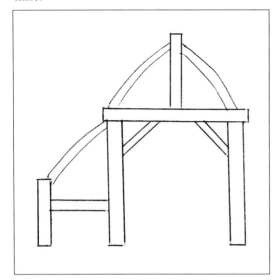

Section of a medieval box framed house with rear aisle of a type common in the Bradford area.

Although the earliest known house on the Horton Hall site has been described as a timber, cruck frame building, in which the weight of roof and walls was supported by pairs of curved timbers joined to form an A shape, this is not born out by photographs taken for the National Monuments Record shortly before demolition after the house had been badly damaged by fire in the 1960s. The construction shown was not a simple curved frame from the ground to the apex of the roof, but appears to have been a box frame of hefty timbers, curving only to form the roof supports. Some of these old timbers were clearly visible within the later house, the original exterior walls being used as internal divisions. Royds Hall at Low Moor, south of Bradford, followed a similar pattern of building and re-building. This house has survived to the present day, and in it massive oak beams dating to about 1300 can clearly be seen. These were part of an external wall, now an internal dividing wall in just the same way as the walls of Horton Hall. William Cudworth stated that the house at Horton was six crooks (crucks) in length, in other words, the length of five bays between the main supports. The entrance hall on the north side of the building remained "low and quaint in appearance, showing the ancient timber supports of very substantial character." There was no standard length for a bay, much depending on the size of timber available, but a scale drawing in the National Monuments Record, extrapolated to allow for later alterations, gives dimensions of approximately 85 feet by 19 feet for the main body of the house, assuming it to have been symmetrical with a central main entrance. In many early medieval houses, the entrance was not central, but had a large hall and private rooms to one side, and smaller service rooms to the other. If this was the layout of the early house, its length would have been more like 65 feet.

No record remains of the interior layout at this time but if it followed a typical pattern for its period and status, a large central hall, or housebody, would have been the chief room and centre of activity. This would most likely have been a single storey room, extending up to the rafters. The "low and quaint" description of the north entrance suggests an aisle running along this side of the building. The aisle might have included a kitchen, but it was not uncommon for cooking to be done in the hall itself. Indoor and outdoor servants would have eaten here as well as the family. Other rooms would have provided some privacy and sleeping accommodation for the family. Originally heating would have been supplied by a central hearth, smoke escaping through a hole in the roof. A portable brazier might have heated other rooms. Some halls had a staircase to a gallery added, giving access to adjacent upstairs rooms, but at the time of a major re-building in 1676, the whole of this house was made two storey. At this stage, if it had not already been done, the fireplace would have been moved to one end and given a chimney.

Although it had a timber frame, the walls were not necessarily a simple lath and plaster construction. Even as early as the fourteenth century, houses of wealthy families in the Bradford area sometimes had stone flags slotted into grooves in the timber uprights, which were then plastered over. The roof would most likely have been Yorkshire flags, needing the very substantial timbers for support.

Thus, while the Sharps were not members of the feudal aristocracy, their house and holding was considerable. They must have been members of the yeoman farmer class that was coming into being as the manorial system with its dependency on serfdom declined. Their name is variously spelled Sharp, Sharpe, Scharp, Scharpe or Scharpp, and the repeated use of Christian names, particularly Christopher, James, John and Thomas, lends some confusion to the oldest known part of the family tree.

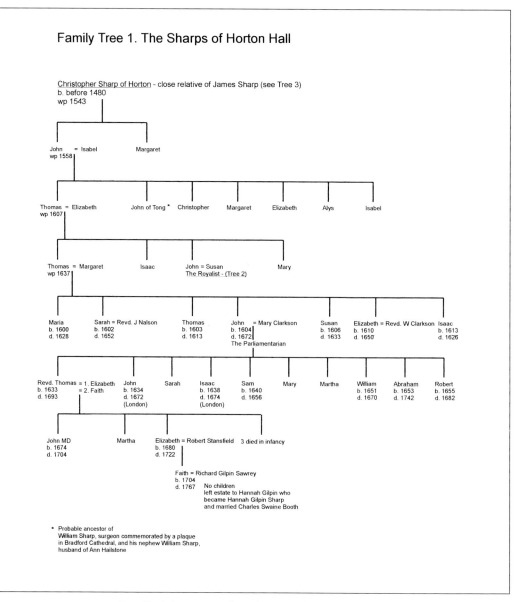

Family Tree 1. The Sharps of Horton Hall

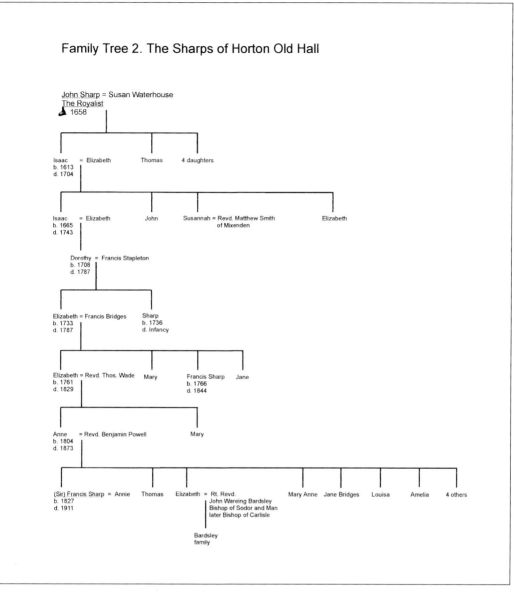

Family Tree 2. The Sharps of Horton Old Hall

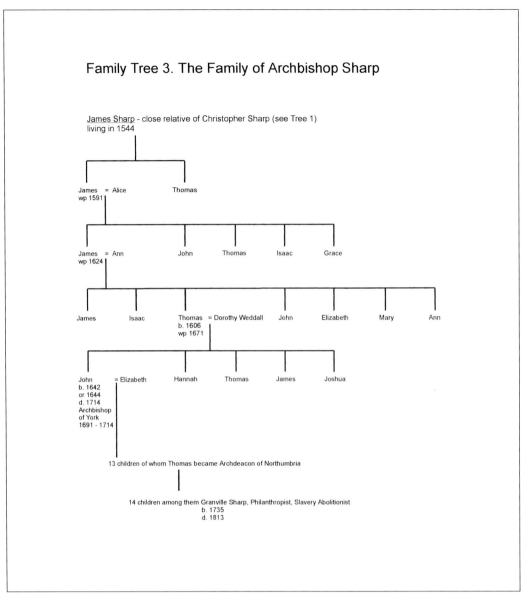

Family Tree 3. The Family of Archbishop Sharp

Chapter 2
Christophers, Jameses, Johns and Thomases!

In 1873 Revd. Joshua Fawcett gave a lecture on the Sharps of Horton Hall, which is quoted in Abraham Holroyd's Collectanea Bradfordiana. He refers to "James Sharp who lived in a house at Horton, late belonging to Kirkstall Abbey." Fawcett goes on to suggest that this was probably the site of the old hall at Little Horton, although, as will become apparent, the term "old hall" could have referred to either of two neighbouring houses. James' possessions were assessed in the 36th year of King Henry VIII (i.e. 1545) at £5. In 1530 he witnessed the will of Christopher Sharp. Also contemporary with James is another Christopher, born some time before 1480 and having a large property at Horton. His assessment, in 1543, the year of his death, was £20, a very considerable sum. His will also was witnessed by James in 1541. Wills were generally witnessed by close family members but whether James was brother, cousin, uncle or nephew to either of the Christophers cannot be determined. The John Sharp, who became Archbishop of York in Queen Anne's reign, is descended from James. Later descendants of the second Christopher have consulted genealogists and the College of Heralds in their attempts to clarify their relationship to the Archbishop. Good pedigrees going back to James and Christopher have been drawn up, and there is no doubt that they were close kin, but nobody has been able to establish the precise relationship between the two. It seems likely that papers which might have clarified the situation could have disappeared during the turmoil of the Civil War.

Revd. Joshua Fawcett said in his lecture that James had four sons. From the first of these, another James, was descended the Archbishop of York, but Fawcett is alone and unsupported in claiming that the second son, John, is the direct ancestor of the Sharps of Horton Hall. Their line can be traced back to that Christopher who died in 1543. Christopher also had a son John, so the confusion is not too surprising.

This John was executor to his father, whose will directed that he should be buried in St. Peter's Church, Bradford. He left money for a trental of Masses (a series of thirty Masses) for his soul and all Christian souls, and eight marks (a mark was worth 13s 4d, two thirds of £1) to his daughter Margaret. John, the only son, succeeded to the estate. John and his wife Isabel had three sons, yet another generation of Thomas, John and Christopher.

John died in 1558, succeeded by his son Thomas, to whom he left "one thing of the best of every kind of vessel accustomed to be occupied at his house at Horton." The Sharp family was growing steadily in wealth and standing, working diligently, like others of their class, and quietly amassing wealth at a time when some, who considered themselves better bred, were finding their fortunes dwindling. Preoccupation with wars and knightly service, to the detriment of managing their estates, had taken its toll on some of the minor nobility, as had unfortunate choices of allegiance during the Wars of the Roses.

Thomas is described as a clothier. This could mean anything from weaving an occasional piece of coarse cloth from local wool spun by his wife Elizabeth, to producing good quality pieces from fine fleeces bought in, perhaps from Lincolnshire, right up to dealing in wool and cloth in all its stages. It is likely that, like other local yeomen, he combined some spinning and weaving by members of his family with farming his land, the cloth business gradually taking precedence. Daniel Defoe, in his "Tour through Great Britain," refers to just such a situation. He says: "At every considerable house was a manufactory.... every clothier must necessarily keep a horse, perhaps two, to fetch home his wool and his provisions from the market, to carry his yarn from the spinners, his manufactures to the fulling mill and to the market to be sold......he keeps a cow or two, or more, for his family."

Bradford was poorly served by roads and had no access to navigable water. Transport of goods was almost entirely by pack horse. This isolation kept Bradford's cloth trade small until the mid 18th century brought enormous growth in both quantity and quality. Turnpike roads passing through Great and Little Horton were opened in 1734, but by this time, the Sharp family had moved into quite a different way of life

In 1558, Thomas inherited not only the best vessels, but also "3 waynes, 2 plowes, 1 harrowe with yoks, tearnes, and other geare to them belonging for husbandrye, as hath been accustomed to be kept at this my howse in Horton." He appears to have added to his land at every opportunity. In 1589, he and three neighbours, Thomas Hodgson of Bolling and Robert Booth and William Field of Horton, had conveyed to them from Richard Lacy, Lord of the Manor of Horton, no less than 250 acres of the unenclosed wastes of Horton and 14 acres lately enclosed. He also bought Bowling Mill Close from Thomas Hodgson for £88. Thomas and Elizabeth Sharp had three sons and a daughter.

Another wealthy Horton family at this time was that of Thomas Wood, whose wife was Richard Lacy's granddaughter. Around the turn of the century, when the Woods disposed of their lands in Horton, Thomas Sharp and his youngest son John bought much of it, some tenanted and yielding rents. In 1602, when John planned to marry Susan, daughter of Richard Waterhouse of Shelf, Thomas re-leased to his son all the property they had bought from the Woods. He had already made over to John several of his other holdings. Richard Waterhouse added property in Shelf and £150. John and Susan made their home very close to Horton Hall.

Thomas and Elizabeth's second son, Isaac, died young. The surviving brothers, Thomas and John were to be the fathers of the two main branches of the Sharps of Little Horton. John now had his own house and land, secured to him in his father's will, and in due course the eldest, Thomas, succeeded to the rest of his father's estate including a list of farm equipment, wagons, ploughs, four yoke of oxen and other necessities, and the principal dwelling house, Horton Hall. Here his wife Martha bore him seven children. Their eldest son lived only to be ten years old, the youngest to thirteen. Two daughters did not survive to adulthood, but Sarah, John and Elizabeth thrived.

The Sharps were still clothiers and farmers, but from their business dealings it is evident that they were educated to a level above that normally associated with those occupations. The marriages of Thomas and Martha's surviving children give a picture of the circles in which the family was moving. Sarah married the Revd. John Nalson, Minister of Holbeck Leeds, and Rector of Walkington. Elizabeth married the Revd. William Clarkson, Rector of Adel, and Thomas's son and heir John married William's sister Mary, twelve years his junior and described by William Cudworth as a woman of considerable culture. The Clarksons were a prosperous Bradford family, living at Fayre Gappe off Westgate. Robert Clarkson, the father of Mary and William, was a manufacturer of woollen cloths and the owner of large estates in and around Bradford. Descendants of his youngest son David took up life in America, and served with distinction both in the colony and later in the emerging independent nation which became the USA.

Chapter 3
Sharps at War

Horton Hall must have been extended and modernised over the years, but expensive and radical re-building was not to take place in that generation or the next.

Thomas Sharp died in 1636. Perhaps he was spared knowledge of the irreconcilably opposing loyalties of his brother and his son, but already by then the conflict between King and Parliament was spreading its dark clouds throughout the land.

The elder John, "Uncle John", was a deeply committed Royalist and took part in several battles fighting for his King. During one engagement he received a severe blow on the head from a battleaxe. In later years he used to say that, but for that blow, he might have lived to be an old man. In spite of it he exceeded his three score years and ten, dying in 1658. He did not live to see the Restoration and never got over the execution of King Charles I. From that terrible day to the end of his life, he never again shaved or cut his hair. His eldest son Isaac was also active in the Royalist cause, commissioned as lieutenant in 1653. He too survived the war, and he it was who built on the site of the family's old house the mansion known as Horton Old Hall. Stages in the building were marked by date stones over various doorways in 1665, 1674 and 1675.

The sympathies of "Uncle John's" nephew and neighbour, young John, rested entirely with the Parliamentary cause. These personal tragedies of divided families were taking place all over England although the part which Bradford played in the Civil War was probably greater than that of any town of its size in the kingdom. General Thomas Fairfax commences his memoirs with the statement: "The first action we had was at Bradford." The historian John James in "The History and Topography of Bradford" in 1841 writes that "the greater part of the nobility, gentry and landed proprietors in the country were on the Royal side. Lord Ferdinando Fairfax of Denton and his son Sir Thomas Fairfax were the only persons of any great consequence who were against the Royal cause. The inhabitants of this locality, however, being principally Puritans, and possessing, from habits of trade, a strong devotion to principals of civil and religious liberty, were in the interest of the Parliament."

In addition to nephew John's own leanings, he had certainly married into a family with a strong Puritan tradition. His father-in-law Robert Clarkson had been a noted Puritan and warden of the Parish Church. His brother-in-law, Elizabeth's husband William, was chaplain to Lord Ferdinando Fairfax. The younger brother-in-law, David Clarkson, came home from his studies at Cambridge to take part in the fighting alongside John Sharp in 1642. William Scruton, in "Pen and Pencil Pictures of Old Bradford" says it is believed that David Clarkson was captured and exchanged for a Royalist prisoner, after which he returned to Cambridge.

The high wall between the properties occupied by the two branches of the Sharp family is said to date from this time.

There have been many books written about the Civil Wars, and Bradford's distinguished nineteenth century historians, John James, William Scruton and William Cudworth all give their accounts. Much of their evidence for local impact comes from Joseph Lister's memoirs. Joseph Lister was an eye witness of several engagements and was at the time apprenticed in the cloth trade to John Sharp the Parliamentarian. He has described how his master was among those who broke out of the besieged town with General Fairfax at the last moment, when it was clear it could no longer be held. Young David Clarkson was one of those who failed to get through. Joseph Lister describes meeting him, leading his horse, after Sharp and the others had broken through the Royalist lines.

"O! What a dreadful night was that in which Bradford was taken! What weeping and wringing of hands! None expected to live longer than till the enemy came in; the Duke of Newcastle having charged his men to kill all - man, woman and child - in the town...."

[The Royalist commander was in fact the Earl of Newcastle, but no doubt Earls and Dukes were all one to an apprentice lad.]

This was the night of the ghostly plea. Whatever the explanation (and there are 'more things in Heaven and Earth') it is a fact that if such a harsh order had been given, the Earl changed it before his army entered the town. Lister says that not more than half a dozen were slain, though there was wholesale pillaging. Afterwards the soldiers sold looted goods back to the townspeople, but were not satisfied even with that degree of exploitation. Lister relates that he was sent by his master's wife, Mary Sharp, to the camp to buy a cow. It was driven away again before night, and another day he went and bought another which was also taken. At least the Sharp household had money to make the purchases. Some would

The Revd. David Clarkson, Brother-in-Law of John Sharp, the Parliamentarian

have lost everything that night.

One can imagine twenty eight year old Mary, soberly dressed, intelligent and capable. She would have servants, farm labourers, apprentices, all looking to her, and she had her five children in the house, the eldest no more than ten years old, the youngest a baby. She would have no means of knowing whether her husband and brothers were alive or dead. Would she have reproached Joseph Lister for not bringing David to the Hall instead of helping him try to find a way out of town? Perhaps not. More likely she applied herself to her prayers and her duty and took upon herself the running of the estate as best she could until better times came. Perhaps they felt reasonably safe at Horton, above the town, although the Royalist camp at Bolling was uncomfortably near. Fortunately for Bradford, the Earl did not remain long, but left a small garrison in the town and withdrew the bulk of his forces to pursue the war in the Midlands.

Portrait of General Sir Thomas Fairfax in Bolling Hall.
By permission of the owners.

Bolling Hall has survived as a museum. It is a larger and grander house than either of the halls at Horton, but spans the same period, with a mixture of building styles. Its rooms, furnished appropriately for the age in which they were built or altered, help to give a picture of life at those times. There is a fine, carved Jacobean bed which was brought from Horton Old Hall shortly before the inglorious end of that fine house in the twentieth century, and may have originally been made for Horton Hall.

Ironically, the "Ghost Room" at Bolling contains no portrait of the Earl of Newcastle, but two of General Thomas Fairfax, which would certainly have spoilt the Earl's sleep, had they been there in 1643. One of these is a nineteenth century painting by W.Dobson, showing a romanticised picture of a robust popular hero with cropped hair and fresh complexion. The other, artist unknown, resembles a contemporary engraving of the General, who was known to be rather small and thin. He is portrayed with shoulder length hair, typical of men of his class on either side of the conflict. From the canvas there looks out a serious, thoughtful, but rather ordinary and unglamorous face. It is tempting to think that his faithful follower John Sharp might have looked something like this, representative of a middle class of industrious, landed families who would infinitely rather not have been at war with their neighbours and even their own kin, but unflinching once convinced where their duty lay.

After the siege of Bradford, John Sharp remained with General Fairfax and was present at the battles of Nantwich and Marston Moor. He became the General's financial secretary and paymaster, a responsible and confidential position. He received two certificates, in 1645 and 1647, for his good service, and a gold medal from Parliament and the City of London, a great honour, only five such medals being struck. Letters from John in 1649 show that he was still engaged in military duties. To his wife Mary he wrote very practically, recommending that their third son, Isaac, should be " put to spin or drive a plow until a master be found for him." He urged the need for good groundwork in arithmetic before going to London - Isaac became a London tradesman.

Chapter 4
Prosperity

John was a merchant as well as a manufacturing clothier, but the textile trade suffered during the wars and was almost extinguished in Bradford. However, his reputation for competence and honesty brought John a role in the service of the Commonwealth. Assessments were levied for the upkeep of the army and navy and John received the post of Collector for a large district in the neighbourhood of Bradford. He was also agent to Sir John Maynard, the Lay Rector of Bradford Parish, and responsible for collecting the manorial tithes.

Despite the troubled times, decline in trade and enforced absences of heads of households, both the Royalist and Parliamentarian branches of the Sharps survived the war with status and wealth apparently undiminished. It is perhaps not surprising that after the Restoration, a loyal Royalist like Lieutenant Isaac Sharp should have been in a position to build Horton Old Hall on the site of his father's old home. This house was an attractive example of its period, consisting of two projecting wings with low pitched gables and between them a recessed housebody with a large mullioned window. Its exterior appearance and the interior of the main hall, with its fine, oak panelled walls and gallery, remained virtually unchanged for almost another three hundred years. Lieutenant Sharp achieved even greater age than his father, living through the reigns of Charles II, James II, William and Mary. He died in 1704 in the second year of the reign of Queen Anne in his ninety first year.

Although William Cudworth described Horton Hall as a fair specimen of an Elizabethan residence, the handsome stone building he so admired was contemporary with its late 17th century neighbour, Jacobean in style, if not strictly so by date. John and Mary's eldest son Thomas began the re-building of his ancestral home in 1676. The first stage was to prepare an agreement with a mason, Nathan Sharp of Wike, for the building of

"one piece of housing adjoining the now dwelling house of Thomas Sharp, about 18 yards or 19 yards in length, seven and a half yards breadth, and about six and a half yards in height at the square."

When Thomas's plans were completed, the medieval building was completely enclosed within an imposing, symmetrical, stone house. On the south front, a porch projected from the centre of a long block with mullioned and transomed windows. Although it was not the main entrance to the house, the porch had an imposing doorway surmounted by a wheel window, one of the largest of its kind, and the latest dated example in the West Riding. Above it, four small circular windows were set in cross formation in a most unusual, possibly unique, lozenge shaped frame. The porch rose above the main roof of the house, forming a square tower. This was later extended upwards and a stone balustrade added, to create an observatory platform for Thomas Sharp's brother Abraham, the distinguished astronomer and mathematician. On either side of the main body of the house were projecting wings, again having stone mullioned and transomed windows. The gables of these wings were of elaborate design of alternating curved and angular sections, topped with stone finials.

The main entrance was through an arched doorway on the north side of the house. This

led in from two courtyards flanked by outbuildings, which in the nineteenth century were combined to form one large courtyard. A fine carved and studded oak door was surmounted by the arms of the Sharps, described in heraldic terms as:

Arms: Azure, a pheon argent, charged with eight torteauxes

Crest: An eagle's head erased, azure, ducally gorged, holding in its mouth a pheon argent.

Motto: Bellicae Virtutis Praemium.

This is a good example of a punning coat of arms. A pheon is the barbed head of a dart or arrow, chosen to illustrate the name Sharp. The growth of the family's holdings in land and property suggests that the early Sharps were indeed sharp, in the sense of being shrewd, and by the seventeenth century it was clear that sharp was an appropriate description of intellect and academic prowess. The family motto, which is a quotation from Livy, translates as "The Reward of Warring Valour." Did Thomas Sharp regard his inheritance as a just reward for his family's virtuous stand and exemplary conduct during the recent war? If so, what must he have thought of the Restoration and the apparently equal prosperity of his Royalist cousin?

A passage led from the north door through to the tower entrance, with rooms off to either side. One of these low rooms, west of the passage, was the servants' hall, known by the Italian name, the Tinello. The loftier rooms on the south front were those used by Thomas Sharp and his family. Stonework of the window in the west wing bore the initials T.S.

Thomas Sharp's original drawings for his new house still survive, having fortuitously been recognised and rescued from the floor of an outbuilding some 175 years later. There is a meticulously drawn ground plan of the proposed new building and several sheets of enlargements of various parts, cross sections and details. Major new walls are clearly shown, and there are alternative proposals for the positioning of windows, stairs and fireplaces. The main plan is covered with tiny, neat writing and columns of figures, referring to "harmonicall proportions", and most detailed measurements of walls, windows, roofing timbers, heights of step risers and so forth. There is even a note about enquiring about the cost of pigs, the necessary size of their housing, how many to get and the cheapest time to buy them.

There is a reference on one page to "Mr. Rawson's house at Shipley", either as a source of design or an example of technique for a particular size of building. William Rawson was Lord of the Manor of Shipley and his family had occupied Shipley Hall, generally known as Shipley Low Hall. This house, although it has lost its setting in extensive grounds, has survived to the present day, partly occupied by Shipley Conservative

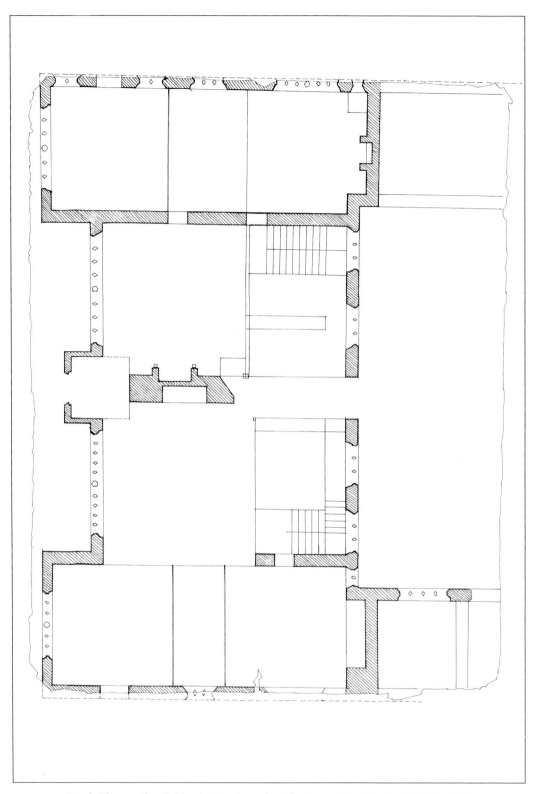

Revd. Thomas Sharp's Plan 1676 redrawn by John Ayres BEng, CEng, MICE, RIBA, ARICS

Association. In 1673, William Rawson built the Manor House, also known as the Over Hall, at the upper corner of Hall Lane at the Windhill side of Shipley. It is described by Cudworth as a spacious building with a noble porch with the initials of William and Mary Rawson on it. It had extensive outbuildings and a large farm attached, possibly the inspiration for Thomas Sharp's venture into pig keeping. It would seem that in the relatively peaceful period of King Charles II's reign, men of means in these parts took the opportunity to improve on the medieval dwellings of their ancestors and set themselves up in the very latest style. Much of the land belonging to Over Hall was sold for the building of houses in the 19th century, and the hall itself has now gone.

Those pages of the Horton Hall plans that are not completely filled with architectural matters were thriftily used up a few years later by Thomas's brother Abraham, with columns of figures headed "Tables of centres and intersections for parallels of declination", "Diameters, Intersections and semi-diameters, Centres", "Tangents of Hours." Some of the masses of figures appear to be logarithmic tables, some are timed astronomical observations. The writing and figures by both Thomas and Abraham are remarkably fine and neat, with very few blots. This may be partly a tribute to the fine quality of Yorkshire quills. Their excellent reputation was such that John Flamsteed, the Astronomer Royal, whose handwriting was a good deal less neat, requested a supply of Yorkshire quills, which Abraham Sharp sent to him by carrier, 2,000 on one occasion, and later a further thousand and a penknife.

Although Thomas was heir to a considerable estate, he was intended for the ordained ministry from an early age. He was born in 1633 and educated first at Bradford Grammar School, then Clare Hall, Cambridge, where his tutor was his uncle, Revd. David Clarkson. What a role model for an intelligent youth of 16, this dashing young uncle, himself only 28, who had interrupted his studies to risk his life in the Parliamentary and Puritan cause. He had fought alongside his pupil's own father, been captured and released in an exchange of prisoners, before returning to Cambridge to achieve his Bachelor of Divinity degree. Another of Thomas's teachers at Cambridge was John Tillotson, a fellow Yorkshireman, later to become Archbishop of Canterbury.

Thomas became an excellent classical scholar and mathematician and gained a Master of Arts degree. He took Holy Orders in 1660, which must have been a source of deep satisfaction to his devout parents. One of Thomas's younger brothers, Sam, was also entered for Clare Hall, and was evidently a young man of great promise, but sadly died at the age of sixteen. Letters from Mary to her sons are full of her religious zeal, but also have such homely touches as their need for new stockings, and the very motherly pleas that they should write to her and their father.

Horton, 23rd October, 1656

Dear Son,

    It is a long time since I heard from you, and many times I am troubled that we cannot hear when Mr. Sturdy goes or comes. If you would not miss of writing by him we should know better how and when to write to you. The last we had was by young Stanhope, which was writ a good while before. I hope you will not fail to write either by our cosen, if you can spare the time, or by Sturdy the first opportunity. I long to hear how it pleases the Lord to carry on his own work in your soule, which to hear would be some refreshment to my drooping spirits, which grones and moanes under a senseless and unprofitable frame of heart under my frownes and corrections, which I cannot find the fruit of as I desired and hoped for. I know it is my sin that procures evill to me and hinders good from me, but I cannot see the great evill that is in sin, nor get my heart affected with it, to lothe myself for it as I should. Oh, that I had faith to believe for that after-fruit, and a heart to indure to the utmost, that I might lose none of that good which the Lord is willing to reach out to His chastened ones. I hope you will not fail in your earnest requests to the Lord that He would please to own our pore soules, and turn to us in mercy, from whom he hath hid his face for a long time, not coming in with those quickenings and refreshings in the enjoyment of His publick ordinances as in times past. Oh, for a heart to cry mightily to Him in private and in secret, as formerly. Oh, what a sad condition hath our sinful divisions brought us into. What can we expect but that some sad judgment is at hand, which is the fear of many. The good Lord fit us for a suffering condition, and help both you and me and all our near relations to make our peace with God, that, what times soever come, we may be found in Christ.

Your father and I will expect you and your brother John next summer, if God grant health and peace. The last letter I had from John he seemed to be under some conviction. I should bless the Lord to hear that it might be carried on to a thorough conversion. I wish when you have opportunity you would put him in mind of that great work of regeneration that we must all pass through before we can enter into life.

If I had known in time that Cosen Wilkinson would have seen you, I would have sent you a pair of gray stockings, but will send them when they are ready. I desire to know what became of brother Sam's linen; it would trouble me to lose it., I mean his sheets and shirts and napkins, for I had provided well for him. If God had given him life he would have wanted no more for a long time, but we were unworthy of such a mercy, and God hath hid him from an evill which I fear is to come. God help us all that are left behind to stand in the gap and to cry mightily for redeeming grace. The good Lord pour out much of his spirit upon you, and make you an able minister of the New Testament, is the earnest prayer of

Your dear mother,
Marie Sharp

In 1660 another young Sharp left Bradford Grammar School and went to Cambridge. This was John Sharp, referred to by a contemporary, Revd. Edmund Calamy, Vicar of St. Mary's, Aldermanbury, London, as Thomas Sharp's cousin. John's great grandfather was James Sharp of Little Horton. His grandfather, another James, lived at Woodhouse in North Bierley, and John's parents, Thomas and Dorothy, had a house in Ivegate, Bradford, where John was born.

John had the Sharp family's enthusiasm for mathematics and science. His biographer A. Tindal Hart wrote: "Newton was now in the ascendant, and Sharp with his clear mathematical brain, which was unfortunately stinted of mathematics and forced into classical and theological grooves, much admired his work, and in after years defended it. He likewise took up botany and chemistry, but had no time to do more than dabble in these subjects."

John took his BA degree in 1663/4, his MA in 1667, and received Holy Orders. Failing to obtain a much desired fellowship at Christ's College, he returned to Bradford. His father had supported him at Cambridge for seven years and now it was necessary for John to earn a living. He applied for the incumbency of Wibsey Chapel - "a mean, thatched building" according to William Cudworth, but was not selected. Had he been appointed to Wibsey, he might well have remained there, struggling on a modest stipend. However, his apparent failure led to an appointment on the recommendation of friends, as chaplain and tutor in an important household, and in due course to his becoming Archbishop of York and a trusted adviser to Queen Anne. Tindal Hart records that it was said that when the Archbishop made a visitation in this part of his diocese, he always placed the incumbent of Wibsey on his right hand at dinner, saying with a degree of pleasantry, that he owed much to him for having stood in his way in former years, and thus prevented his settling down in a humble sphere and a retired district where he might never have been known.

The Revd. Thomas Sharp, leaving Cambridge in 1660, served a curacy in Peterborough until, on the death of his uncle William Clarkson, he was presented to the living of Adel. He was not to enjoy this for long, because after the Restoration, Dr. Hick of Guiseley challenged the appointment, claiming the living on the grounds of having been ejected. Thomas resigned and could have sought another living, but felt unable to subscribe to the Act of Uniformity of 1662. This required from the clergy a declaration of unfeigned assent and consent to everything contained in the Prayer Book and a declaration to conform to "the Liturgy of the Church of England as it is now by law established." He retired to his father's house at Horton, then went to Reading. In 1668 he married Elizabeth Bagnall, but she and their infant daughter died less than two years later.

In 1672, Thomas's father John died at the age of 68 and Thomas returned to the considerable estate he inherited. That same year, King Charles II allowed Nonconformists to apply for licences for the holding of religious services. Thomas obtained a licence for Horton Hall, the first, but not the last time that religious services were to be held in the house. Here he exercised his ministry and great numbers flocked to hear him.

John's will lists houses and closes of land throughout Great and Little Horton and a notebook left by Revd. Thomas, referred to by William Cudworth, shows how he administered the estate, valued at £1790 - 15s. He paid various debts and legacies - his brother Isaac's portion, and later that same Isaac's funeral expenses, John's portion, Martha's portion, and apprenticeship money for brothers William and Abraham.

In 1673 he married Faith, the daughter of another notable Nonconformist minister, the Revd. James Sale of Pudsey. Thomas and Faith had several children, but only two, John and Elizabeth, survived to adulthood. Another daughter, Martha, is mentioned in Thomas's will, but is thought to have predeceased him, or at least died before adulthood. The will stated that, "the houses and lands bequeathed to my two daughters be at the sole management of my dear wife for their education."

After some years of ministry in Horton, Thomas accepted a call to the Independent Chapel at Morley and then to Mill Hill Chapel in Leeds. He fitted out a house in Leeds but also continued to live at Horton Hall, now magnificently rebuilt. The house at Leeds must also have been substantial since an inventory of goods and chattels shows the contents of Horton Hall to be valued at £149-18s, and those of the Leeds house £134-17-4d.

A selection from the Horton Hall inventory gives some idea of the standards of comfort and elegance enjoyed:

In the Dining Room	£	s	d
1 round table and carpet	2	10	0
1 square table and 1 seeing glass	2	0	0
12 chairs with backs, 2 seats set work	4	10	0
6 arch chairs, covered with set work	1	10	0
4 pictures, large map, and weather glass	6	0	0
In the Best Chamber			
12 arch chairs and 1 table	2	11	0
1 pair bedstocks, 1 feather bed, and bedding with hangings	5	0	0
6 chairs covd. with set work, and couch chair	4	10	0
1 buffet and stool, 1 screen	0	13	0

but perhaps the most interesting section of the list is that for the study, showing the priority the Sharps placed on learning. More than half the total value of the household goods are to be found here:

In the Study			
4 maps that hang up, a colln. of other maps, and the library	80	0	0

Thomas was celebrated as a writer as well as a preacher. "Divine Comforts, Antidoting Inward Perplexities" enjoyed a wide circulation, and he also wrote poetry.

On 4th August 1693, he rode to Leeds to preach and was stricken with pleurisy. He

HORTON HALL AS IT WAS.

Horton Hall in the 18th Century.

cannot have been able to return to Horton, for on August 27th he died, and was buried in Leeds. Edmund Calamy said of him "He was every way a great man, and yet clothed with humility. He was very laborious in his work, full of self-denial, exceeding temperate and mortified to all earthly enjoyments, and of a peaceable, catholic spirit. His sermons were elaborate and accurate; and all his performances were exceeding polite and scholar-like."

The house at Leeds Towne End was among the property left to "my beloved wife, Faith Sharp, to be sold for the discharge and payment of my lawful debts." Faith lived at Horton Hall for the rest of her life. She died in 1710 at the age of 59.

Thomas and Faith's son John was another scholar of scientific leaning. He went to Holland to study medicine at Leyden, completing his studies in 1699. Dr. Sharp's untimely death in 1704, when he was only thirty years old, must have been a sad blow to his widowed mother. He was unmarried, and on his death the estate eventually passed to his father's younger brother Abraham.

Horton Old Hall, home of the Royalist Sharps.

Chapter 5
"The Incomparable Mr. Sharp"

Abraham Sharp, born in 1653, was to prove the most distinguished member of a family remarkable for scholarship, diligence and integrity. William Cudworth, in his "Life and Correspondence of Abraham Sharp", gives a detailed account of Abraham's life and work.

He was educated first at the village school in Horton, then, following in the footsteps of his brother Thomas and their 'cousin' John (the future Archbishop), at Bradford Grammar School. This school, which had already been in existence for more than 200 years, was at this time situated just to the west of the parish churchyard, in what was eventually to become Forster Square. Here his love of mathematics developed, and by implication, his skill in Latin. Would-be mathematicians were obliged to become competent Latin scholars, whether they liked it or not, since the school's mathematics text books were in that language.

John Sharp (the Parliamentarian) did not have an academic career in mind for this younger son and Abraham did not follow the older boys to Cambridge. Instead, at the age of sixteen he was apprenticed to William Shaw, a mercer, or dealer in textiles, in York. An apprentice-master was not only an employer and instructor, but stood very much in loco

Abraham Sharp

parentis. Terms of the apprenticeship might have been frustrating for many a young man out of range of his father's supervision for the first time:

"fornication in the house of his said master nor without, he shall not commit; taverns of custom he shall not haunt, unless it be about his said master's business there to be doing; at cards, dice, or any other unlawful games he shall not play."

Nor might the apprentice marry without his master's consent, although by the end of the eight year term for which he was bound, Abraham would have been twenty four.

It is unlikely that any of these conditions would have irked the studious young Puritan, but he could raise no enthusiasm for the cloth trade and longed only to pursue his scientific learning. He very soon parted company with William Shaw, possibly to their mutual relief, but did not go home to face his father's displeasure. Abraham made his way to Liverpool and supported himself by opening a school, teaching writing and accounts, while he studied navigation and mathematics.

The circumstances in which he met John Flamsteed, who became the first English Astronomer Royal in 1675, are unknown, but Cudworth relates the traditional version:

The Revd. John Flamsteed, the first Astronomer Royal

"Tradition has it that Flamsteed was at the time residing in the house of a merchant in London, with whom Sharp became acquainted while he was on a visit to Liverpool, and that in order to be brought into contact with one so gifted in astronomical research, Sharp engaged himself as bookkeeper to the merchant, and so got to London."

What is certain is that he was in Flamsteed's employment by 1684. A letter from Flamsteed to Sharp at Little Horton dated 20 Sept. 1710 states, "you lived with me in 1684 and 1685", and goes on to refer to astronomical observations taken at that time. Abraham kept meticulous notes of all his income and expenditure and it is apparent that between 1684 and 1690 he was receiving modest payment from Flamsteed. He was also getting financial help from his own family because the allowance made by the Government to the Astronomer Royal was too small to allow him to pay an assistant adequately. Abraham's father had died by this time, and the money came from brother Thomas and a cousin by marriage, Robert Clarkson.

The Observatory at Greenwich was opened in 1676, but run on such a shoestring that it was only when Flamsteed inherited family property that he was able to improve the quality of its instruments.

The most significant of these was the Mural Arc, vital for the Astronomer Royal's observations leading to the eventual publication of his "Catalogue of Fixed Stars." The making and calibrating of this instrument was the work of Abraham Sharp. Oxford

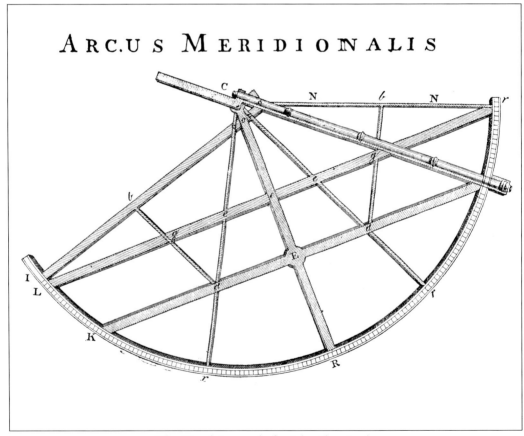

The Mural Arc made for John Flamsteed.

historian Allan Chapman, in his book "Dividing the Circle - The Development of Critical Angular Measurement in Astronomy 1500-1850", says of this achievement, "After enduring nearly fifteen years of frustration caused by inadequate instruments at Greenwich, Flamsteed acquired in Sharp's arc the finest and most exact astronomical instrument constructed to date, and it won the praise of all who saw it." It took fourteen months to build and cost £120. Flamsteed gives a detailed description in his "Historia Coelestis", concluding: "The making of this was principally the work of Abraham Sharp, my most trusty assistant, a man enriched with gifts and resources of every kind to render him competent to complete a work so intricate and difficult.."

Flamsteed's great work, the "Historia Coelestis Britannica", which included the catalogue of stars, was still unpublished at his death in 1719, partly due to disagreement between the Astronomer Royal and Edmund Halley and Sir Isaac Newton, including accusations about unauthorised publication of parts of the manuscript. Sharp, with Flamsteed's last assistant, Joseph Crosthwait, undertook all necessary revisions, calculations and drawings and put in a huge amount of time and effort to ensure its publication. Margaret Flamsteed, the astronomer's widow, expressed her great gratitude in a letter to Sharp but, for unknown reasons, made no reference to him or Crosthwait in the dedication of the book to King George I. This was signed by her and James Hodgson as nominal editors. (Hodgson had also been an assistant at the Observatory and had married Flamsteed's niece.)

Dr. Chapman has acknowledged Sharp's contribution to the fast growing science of astronomy. Summarising the situation in 1678 he says, "The telescopic sight was rich with both optical and mechanical possibilities, which required only the craftsmanship of Abraham Sharp and George Graham (a London instrument maker,1675-1752) to transform into physical realities." He includes in his book details of the instrument and the data it made it possible for Flamsteed to establish, much of which was supplied to Isaac Newton. Newton's failure to acknowledge his contributions was a source of annoyance to Flamsteed, to which he refers in his correspondence with Abraham Sharp. Dr. Chapman states that, "When the last recorded observation with the mural arc was made, shortly before Flamsteed's death on December 31st 1719, the foundation had been laid for the 'astronomy of exactitude' that was to become the hallmark of 18th century scientific achievement."

Cudworth states that Sharp remained with Flamsteed at Greenwich until 1690, assisting with the observations and cataloguing of nearly 3000 fixed stars. In November of that year, he moved from Greenwich and rented rooms from William Court at the Mariner and Anchor on Little Tower Hill. Mathematical books and instruments were sold here and it is possible that Abraham taught mathematics. A letter home to brother Thomas shows that he was struggling to make a living, business, (whether by teaching or instrument making is not specified) being poorer than he had hoped for, due to the effect of the war. It was a troubled time for England, with conflict in Ireland and on the Continent. Abraham had been offered a position in Portsmouth, which he was reluctant to take up, Portsmouth being notorious for its unhealthy air. However, in February 1691 he made the move. Entries in his notebooks show that he held a position in the King's shipyard as well as receiving a salary from a Mr. Graham, for whom he may have made nautical instruments. He also made mathematical and astronomical instruments, and taught navigation.

He stayed for two years, then items in his notebook refer to his return:

"Came to London, Feb.1st, 1693, and lodged at night at the White Horse, Cripplegate. Had 7 boxes and 2 trunks.

9 nights' lodging at the White Horse, 3/-, fire 6d, Sunday dinner 10d, chamber maid 1/-, 5s.4d.

Sent to Bradford per John Hall six trunks, weighs forty stone.

Came to Little Horton, March 29, 1694."

So Abraham came home. It is impossible to know why he left Greenwich, certainly not because of any lessening in regard between himself and the Astronomer Royal, for these two maintained a correspondence for the next twenty years. Cudworth speculates that his health was not good, possibly affected by long nights of work at the Observatory. It may be that with the completion of the mural arc, the assistant's role no longer called for Sharp's particular skills. The move to Portsmouth was obviously for financial reasons, but we cannot know why he stayed so short a time. Perhaps he felt the northern climate would suit him better. Letters during the London years show him and his brother on affectionate terms - perhaps he was simply homesick for home and family.

If that were the case, it was a sad homecoming. Faith Sharp may have sent for her brother-in-law when Thomas fell ill, or after his death, but the dispatch of a trunk in February 1693 does suggest that Abraham was already planning to go back to Horton. Whatever the plan, before his arrival in March 1694, Thomas had contracted the illness that carried him off in the space of only three weeks.

Shortly after his return to Horton, Abraham received letters from leading mathematicians of the day, urging him to apply for the post of Mathematical Master at Christ's Hospital and return to London. John Flamsteed and Edmund Halley were among those willing to support his application. All speak highly of his ability and Halley's letter refers to a piece of work of his own which Sharp had improved on - "to so good a purpose that I cannot believe it can be carried further, and I congratulate you on your happy discovery."

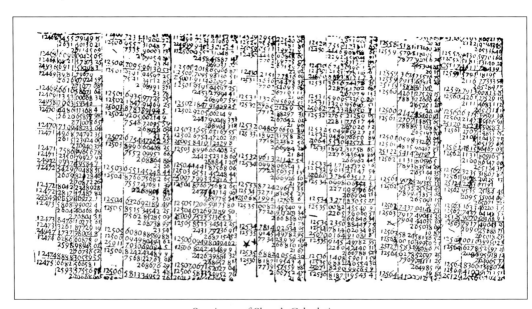

Specimen of Sharp's Calculations

Abraham showed no inclination to leave Horton and he now had an additional reason of duty to stay. The new master of the estate was his young nephew John, who was keen to continue his studies. Abraham took upon himself the management of the family property. Letters of Attorney from John in 1699 authorised "my well beloved Uncle" to collect rents and other dues. This would seem to have been a totally unselfish act of family responsibility, for Abraham can have had no thought of inheriting. The expectation must have been that once he was qualified and set up in medical practice, John would marry and raise a family. Nor was it a means of having a free roof over his head, for Abraham paid his sister-in-law for his board.

He had a study on the first floor, furnished with a small oak desk, which was reputed to have cavities on its surface worn by the astronomer's elbows. A window provided light for the desk and the opposite wall was lined with bookshelves for a considerable library, protected by a railing. The room was oak panelled and a flight of steps ran upwards from one corner to the tower. Thomas Sharp's central porch was heightened by a storey and extended backwards above the roof of the main building.

Nikolaus Pevsner dates this extension at 1694, just after Thomas's death. Abraham Sharp did not own Horton Hall at this time, but young Dr. Sharp shared his uncle's love of science and it is quite possible that he would have been perfectly agreeable to having this work carried out. The date 1712 stamped on the lead of the porch roof might suggest this as an alternative date for the tower observatory. This would tie in with a letter from Sharp to Flamsteed in 1703, telling of observations made from a window or the grounds:

"The last year Jupiter ran not so high but I could without difficulty observe him within doors at a casement, but this year he has got quite above my reach, so that I have been constrained to attend him without doors. For some time had the convenience of resting my telescope on some old apple trees in an adjoining orchard, by the help of which I made a tolerable shift, but since my nephew, after his return from Leyden, designing to bring the garden into better order, has cut them all down, I have been forced to contrive and make a large tripod, or three-legged staff, about 8 or 9 feet high, of strength sufficient to support the tube I use, which is 16 feet long, by which I can raise and turn it with little trouble, but have not yet a screw frame whereon to rest the other end, which I cannot procure here but must be forced to make."

Abraham did indeed make most of the equipment he used, even grinding some of his lenses himself. When necessary he made the tools with which to make his scientific instruments. Among his practical inventions was an accurate odometer or "way-wiser". This could be fitted to a carriage wheel and would keep an exact account of the distance travelled in miles and chains and yards. Abraham tested it by measuring the distance to several places in his own neighbourhood. He sold one to the Archbishop of York for five guineas and offered to send one to Flamsteed, "if such a wheel may be advantageous or valuable to you, should willingly make and send you one, accepting only your book and maps of the stars in satisfaction for it."

Flamsteed replied that he was neither wealthy enough to keep a coach, nor so infirm as to need one, but assured his friend that when he did, he would have no way-wiser but that designed and made by Sharp.

William Cudworth refers to a fine orrery by Sharp, in the museum at York. There is an orrery in the Castle Museum which may be the very one, but it bears no maker's name and

Abraham Sharp's Telescope now at the National Maritime Museum, Greenwich.
(© National Maritime Museum, London)

The Abraham Sharp Exhibit at Life Force. (Photo: A. Hansen)

the museum has no record of its provenance.

Few of Sharp's fine instruments have survived. The Science Museum in London has a beautifully engraved calculating device known as the universal quadrant and the National Maritime Museum at Greenwich has a five foot mural quadrant arc. Many years after Abraham Sharp's death this was rescued in the nick of time by the Revd. N. S. Heineken from a brazier who wanted to buy it to melt down the brass for mending kettles. Mr. Heineken gave the instrument to the Royal Observatory, a most fitting home for it. The National Maritime Museum also has a double refracting telescope, on loan from the Yorkshire Museum.

John Smeaton (1724-92), of Whitkirk, Leeds, the constructor of the Eddystone lighthouse, who was himself a mathematical instrument maker, paid tribute to Sharp's skill in a letter quoted by Cudworth. After praising Sharp's skill in designing and constructing the mural arc at Greenwich, Smeaton goes on to say,

"I have been the more particular relating to Mr. Sharp, in the business of constructing this mural arc, not only because we may suppose it the first good and valid instrument of the kind, but because I look upon Mr. Sharp to have been the first person that cut accurate and delicate divisions upon astronomical instruments, of which, independent of Mr. Flamsteed's testimony, there still remains considerable proofs; for after leaving Mr. Flamsteed and quitting the department above mentioned, he retired to the village of Little Horton, near Bradford, Yorkshire, where I have seen not only a large and very fine collection of mechanical tools, the principal ones being made with his own hands, but also a great variety of scales and instruments made with them, both in wood and brass, the divisions of which are so exquisite as would not discredit the first artists of the present times. "

The workshop in which these fine instruments were produced was in one of the wings on the north side of the hall, overlooking the large courtyard. Abraham's bedroom adjoined it and a passage led to his study and the observatory tower. The door to the study was approached by three steps, but it was a door by which few were allowed to enter. In order not to be interrupted, Abraham had a sliding panel made in a cavity near the doorway. Here his household servants were instructed to place his meals silently. When absorbed in calculations, he would be oblivious of time or hunger and often whole day's meals were found untouched. There is a story recounted by John James in "The History and Topography of Bradford" (1841) that on one occasion he was so absorbed in the solution of a profound mathematical problem that he neglected his meals for an alarming period. His friends were induced, contrary to his prohibitions, to go in on the third day. He complained, though with his accustomed mildness, that they had disarranged a series of investigations which it had cost him three days to form, and that he would have to begin the work nearly anew.

1704 saw a tragedy that marked the beginning of the end for the Sharps of Horton and was a source of pain for Abraham. On January 22nd he wrote to Flamsteed, "...it is with much trouble and discomposure that I now write. It has pleased God to take out of this world my nearest kinsman and only nephew, a young man ever hopeful, in the flower of his age, who had a few years ago been a student of physic at Leyden. A good proficient for his time, just beginning to practise, of good parts and solid judgements. The only son of a most disconsolate mother, him on whom the hopes of a family depended which has continued here in the name above 500 years - now likely to be extinct - the only person here with whom I could have any agreeable converse."

Abraham's description of Dr. John as his only nephew is at odds with the suggestion by Cudworth, and found in some dictionaries of biography, that Thomas Ramsden, father of the celebrated instrument maker Jesse Ramsden was a nephew of Abraham Sharp. Scientific biographers researching the life of Jesse Ramsden have been unable to find any marriage certificates or other records to link the names of Ramsden and Sharp. If there was a relationship, it must have been more distant, although it is an attractive theory, given the character of Jesse, who was born in 1735 at Salterhebble near Halifax. He was apprenticed to a clothworker, but, like Abraham Sharp, he transferred himself to the field of mathematical instrument making. His agreeable nature, simple habits and disregard of the need to eat or sleep while engaged on a project are quite reminiscent of the Horton astronomer.

Abraham's loss was not only of a much loved relation, but of a scientifically educated friend. That there were not many in the Bradford area who could fill that gap is indicated in correspondence with Flamsteed in which Sharp laments that he could find no one whom he could instruct in the use of his instruments. However he was not a total recluse and there were friends who were gladly received at Horton Hall. Cudworth describes the strange ritual by which visitors could find out whether they were welcome. Sharp was almost invariably cloistered in his study and the visitor must rub a stone against the outside of the door. If the moment was appropriate and the scholar in the mood for company, the door would be opened. It would be out of character for this gentle and generous man to be deliberately rude to those who had taken the trouble to visit him and the purpose of the strange system must have been to prevent many hours of complex calculations being lost by interruption of concentration or a train of thought. An engraving of Abraham, with a hint of a smile and a sparkle of amusement in his eyes, gives rise to the notion that a boyish sense of fun might also come into play. Perhaps a half jesting scheme of codes and secret signals was a source of entertainment to the mathematician.

Those who did enjoy friendly and learned conversation at Horton Hall included Dr. Swaine, an apothecary, of Hall Ings, Dr. Richardson of Bierley and Mr. Ralph Thoresby of Leeds, author of "Ducatus Leodiensis or Topography of Leeds." Nonconformist ministers were also welcome visitors at the hall, as in Abraham's brother the Revd. Thomas's time, notably Revd. Oliver Heywood and two younger ministers who both had some interest in mathematics, Revd. Eli Dawson and Revd. Nathaniel Priestley. A sundial was discovered in Leeds in the 19th century bearing the inscription:

FUGIT HORA : ORA LABORA   (Time flies : pray and work)
      Nath. Priestley, calculavit.
      Abr. Sharp, delineavit.
      Latit 55-15   1722.

(calculated by Nathaniel Priestley, delineated by Abraham Sharp)

Abraham himself was an adherent of the Nonconformist brand of Christianity, a strict Presbyterian, though evidently not a strict teetotaller, as several entries for cherry brandy in his household accounts testify.

He attended the chapel in Horton, at Chapel Green, Thornton Lane. This was the first Nonconformist meeting room to be built in Horton, on land thought to have been given by Revd. Thomas Sharp. Eli Dawson was for some time the minister there.

In 1719, a Presbyterian Chapel for Bradford was opened in Chapel Lane, just within the boundary of Horton township. This site was given by Robert Stansfield of Bradford, who had married Revd. Thomas Sharp's daughter Elizabeth, and was part of the land known as Murgatroyd's Croft which his wife had inherited from her father. Abraham was a trustee of this chapel and a generous donor to its building fund. Entries in his notebook show a liberality in his donations for religious purposes, with money for this chapel next to donations to Mr. Kennet, Vicar of Bradford Parish Church. The Civil War divisions seem not to have led to a lasting rift in the Sharp family, for Abraham also gave money to Isaac, the son of his cousin Lieutenant Isaac Sharp of Horton Old Hall, for the building of a meeting place for his son-in-law Revd. Matthew Smith who founded the Nonconformist Chapel at Mixenden, Halifax.

One of Abraham's more eccentric means of charitable giving was his custom of walking to chapel, holding behind his back a handful of coins, so that any needy neighbour could help himself unseen.

It is no reflection on Bradford's professional classes that Abraham lacked companions at his own academic level, but rather a measure of his quite outstanding gifts and abilities. The correspondence studied and published by William Cudworth makes it clear that he was held in the highest regard by the most distinguished men of his time. What chiefly sets him apart from them is his removal from the Capital, with its intrigues and rivalries, to the obscurity and peace of Little Horton.

The mathematical puzzle of "squaring the circle" had been attracting the best endeavours of the mathematicians of Europe, and a Dutchman, Ludolph van Ceulen, had produced a solution in 1596 giving the value of pi to 20 places of decimals. In 1621 he produced a value to 35 decimal places. This achievement was hailed among mathematicians, bringing fame to van Ceulen in his lifetime, the process of the work even being engraved on his tomb. In 1699 Abraham Sharp, for his own amusement, calculated the quadrature to 72 places. He had intended it for private circulation among friends, but Flamsteed judged it so worthy of publication that he personally organised and paid for it. Edmund Halley, in a paper to the Royal Society entitled "An Easy Quadrature of the Circle" wrote that,

"Since van Ceulen's time there had been many abortive essays towards a perfect quadrature. Much had been done towards facilitating the calculus by methods far differing from that of Archimedes, and particularly the doctrine of fluxions, and of infinite series, which might not improperly be called the Geometry of Curve-lines invented by Sir Isaac Newton, which afforded many solutions of the problem. The problem had tempted the ready pen of the most incomparable Mr. Sharp, who had contrived to double the famous numbers of van Ceulen, a degree of exactness far surpassing all belief."

Abraham calculated a table of natural and logarithmic sines, tangents and secants to every second in the first minute of a degree. He was a contributor to the Mathematical Tables compiled in 1705 by the mathematician Henry Sherwin, the other contributors being Mr. Henry Briggs, Dr. Wallis and Dr. Halley, all Savilian Professors of Geometry in the University of Oxford. The book was dedicated to Dr. Halley and the dedicatory letter, paying tribute to all the contributors, includes "Mr. Abra. Sharp, the wonder of the last and present age for industry of this kind."

Abraham also produced a highly acclaimed book, "Geometry Improved", its author modestly described simply as A.S., Philomath.

Cudworth quotes a story current at the time of his researches, that Mr. Sharp "on one occasion, not being able to solve a mathematical problem he was intent upon, and having heard that some person in Scotland was clever at such studies, he made the journey thither to see him. Finding out the object of his search, he narrated his errand, when he was told that there was only one man who could help him, and that he had better seek him out. Sharp asked who it was, when the Scotchman, in perfect ignorance as to the name of his visitor, said that his name was Abraham Sharp, and that he lived at Little Horton, near Bradford!"

Some of the correspondence between Sharp and Flamsteed touches on the important problem of accurately determining longitude at sea. This was a matter of enormous concern to all maritime nations and had led to terrible losses of men and ships. For England, the single most disastrous incident had been the loss, in 1707, of four of the five ships of Admiral Sir Clowdisley Shovell's victorious fleet off the Scillies when almost home. The primary purpose for which the Royal Observatory was founded was to pursue astronomical methods of determining longitude. In 1714, the Longitude Act established a substantial prize for an accurate solution. This stimulated a vast number of suggestions, some from eminent and learned men, others decidedly eccentric in nature. Sharp could not see how anyone could be successful without the help of more accurate astronomical tables than existed in 1714, and he felt sure that the eventual solution must depend on Flamsteed's tables of fixed stars and planets which still awaited publication. When the reward of up to

£20,000 was offered, Flamsteed was appointed one of the Commissioners to receive submissions and report on them. He entertained his friend with accounts of some of the more improbable proposals. These included attempts to produce a pendulum clock mounted in such a way that it would not be affected by the motion of the ship and an aquatic version of a way-wiser which would ride over the waves. Flamsteed touched on the proposal by mathematicians William Whiston and Humphrey Ditton to calculate a ship's position by means of its distance from points from which a gun shot might be heard. " I am sorry for them," he wrote, " and shall tell you no more of them but order their book to be sent this week to London, to be sent to you." These two were renowned mathematicians, Ditton holding the post at Christ's Hospital which Sharp had declined to pursue. Unfortunately their knowledge of mathematics was not matched by their understanding of what was feasible at sea.

The actual solution was eventually to be achieved by another painstaking Yorkshireman, John Harrison, a self-taught clock maker, son of a carpenter on the Nostell Priory estate.

In 1710, Abraham's sister-in-law Faith died. She left property at Farsley, Wheatley, Stead, Burley-in-Wharfedale and Horsforth to Abraham, to pass on his death to his niece, her daughter Elizabeth Stansfield until Elizabeth's daughter Faith should reach the age of 21. She stipulated that Elizabeth, Faith and her heirs should make a yearly payment to the preaching minister of Horton Chapel and also that they "distribute and pay yearly during such tymes as the capital messuage at Horton, wherein I now dwell, shall be uninhabited by the owners thereof, the yearly sum of forty shillings amongst the poor of the town of Horton, yearly, in the winter season, according to the discretion of my brother Abraham Sharp, during his lifetime, and after his decease according to their own discretion."

This suggests that Faith Sharp was confident that while the family were living in Horton Hall they would fulfil their duty towards the poor of the township. She was concerned that they might suffer if the Hall, passing through the female line, was no longer the principal residence of the family.

Abraham too made provision for the chapel and the local poor in his will, leaving to the chapel trustees five volumes of the first edition of Matthew Henry's Exposition of the Old and New Testaments. He also left a small estate he had purchased from Christopher Jackson, the principal house to be a dwelling for the Minister and his family, and the rents from the estate to provide bread "to be distributed every Lord's Day at the Dissenters' Chapel to poor people who attend constantly."

Elizabeth and Robert Stansfield had six sons and two daughters of whom only Faith survived. So young Faith Stansfield, granddaughter of Faith and Rev. Thomas Sharp, great niece of Abraham, was now heiress of Horton Hall and all its estates. Abraham took a great interest in her well being and her education at Mr. Hotham's School at York.

In 1722 Abraham's niece Elizabeth died. In that same year, Faith, now 18, married Richard Gilpin Sawrey of Horton and Broughton Tower, Lancashire. The young couple made their home at Horton Hall with Uncle Abraham. They travelled a great deal, going sometimes to Broughton and often to Cumberland where Richard Sawrey had business interests. Letters were exchanged during these travels, Abraham showing a tender concern for his great niece's health. While at Horton, Richard Sawrey acted as agent for Abraham Sharp, dealing with tenants and collecting rents. When the young couple were away, Abraham looked after their interests in Horton, including Richard Sawrey's commitments to the Presbyterian Chapel. Their relationship is expressed in a letter from Richard Sawrey to Abraham Sharp concerning disagreements at the chapel over a change of minister. The letter ends,

"But I submit all these things to your consideration, and as I have given you the authority of a father over me I shall obey your commands with all dutifulness, and to act in conjunction with my wife, or those that fill the places of Mrs. Sharp and Mrs. Stansfield, without whose generous assistance and yours, there would never have been a chapel at Bradford. Your most dutiful and much obliged nephew, R.G.Sawrey."

Some accounts of Abraham Sharp refer to his physical weakness and yet he lived into his 90th year. It would be wrong, or at least incomplete, to remember him as the eccentric old recluse of Horton. This would be to forget his youthful initiative in leaving his apprenticeship, getting himself from York to Liverpool and supporting himself there by his own efforts. It would be to overlook his life in the Capital, working at the leading edge of mathematical skill and mixing with some of the greatest scientific minds of the day. It would be to forget the significance of his work for the Astronomer Royal and its contribution to the development of astronomy. This importance in the development of astronomy has been acknowledged in a most fitting way by the naming of features on the bright side of the moon. Here he is in perpetual company with Flamsteed and Newton. Sharp's rille, or cleft, and a large crater bearing his name are to be found just to the west of the Sinus Iridum, the Bay of Rainbows.

During his long life, his mathematics and science continued to win him the admiration of leading scientists. Equally renowned was his practical skill in the making of many fine instruments. He took personal day to day interest in the estates he managed on his own behalf and for the benefit of other members of the family. Not least, he was active in pursuit of his Christian faith, greatly furthering the cause of Nonconformists while maintaining an amicable relationship with the Parish Church.

In this church he was laid to rest on July 21st 1742. There is an imposing memorial tablet carved by P.Scheemaker on the wall of the north aisle of what is now Bradford Cathedral. The Latin inscription translates as follows:

Here lie buried the mortal remains of ABRAHAM SHARP descended from an ancient family and united by the tie of blood relationship to the Archbishop of York of that name; who was justly reckoned amongst the most skilful Mathematicians of his time, and was intimate with those of his contemporaries who were distinguished by the same renown, especially with Flamsteed and the illustrious Newton. He illustrated the astronomy of the former by diagrams, with the greatest accuracy; he published also anonymously various writings, and descriptions of instruments constructed by himself. When he had spent a quiet and useful unmarried life in these studies, remarkable for his piety towards God, his kindness to the poor, and his benevolence to all men; at last, in the ninety first year of his age, replete with earthly knowledge, he passed to Heaven. July 18th 1742.

(The reference to his 91st year is due to the mistaken belief that he was born in 1651. His Baptism entry in the Parish Church register is June 1st 1653.)

With Abraham's death, the male line of the Sharps of Horton Hall came to an end. Only a year later, the name of Sharp was similarly lost to Horton Old Hall when Isaac died on 29th July 1743, to be succeeded by his daughter Dorothy, who married Francis Stapleton.

Chapter 6
A Gentleman's Residence

Faith Sawrey duly inherited Horton Hall and other properties from her Great Uncle Abraham and her Grandmother Faith Sharp, but the Sawreys had no children and when Faith died in 1767, the estate was left to her niece by marriage, Hannah Gilpin. Hannah came originally from Whitehaven but was already living at Horton with her Aunt.

Faith Sawrey was the last direct blood descendant of the Horton Hall Sharps to occupy the Hall, but Hannah adopted the name of her Aunt's family, and it was as Hannah Gilpin Sharp that in 1769 she married Charles Swaine Booth. Charles was a barrister-at-law, the son of Revd. Charles Booth of Bradford who had married a daughter of William Swaine, also of Bradford. Another member of the family, Abraham Sharp's friend Dr. Swaine, lived at Hall Ings with his unmarried sister, who left her property to her nephew Charles, at which time he added the name of Swaine. Charles Swaine Booth thus acquired the property of both Booths and Swaines.

Middle class obsession with suitable alliances, bringing wealth and/or status, following the pattern long set by the nobility, probably reached a peak in the late18th and 19th centuries. When Charles married Hannah, he added very considerably to his possessions and even though his bride was scarcely a Sharp herself, the name was a distinguished one, and

Horton Hall with Charles Swaine Booth Sharp's Extension
(from the Blunt family photographs)

the new master of Horton Hall styled himself Charles Swaine Booth Sharp. He was the only Bradfordian to have streets named after all three of his fore-names. Charles Street, Booth Street and Swaine Street were all in the area between Market Street and Hall Ings. Only Charles Street survived 1960s redevelopment of the city centre.

In another branch of the family, the name of Sharp was equally prized by another bridegroom. Catharine Sharp was the niece of John, Archdeacon of Northumberland, granddaughter of Thomas, Archdeacon of Northumberland, and great granddaughter of John, Archbishop of York. A monument in Bamburgh Parish Church describes her as the sole survivor of the name. When she married the Revd. Andrew Bowlt, he too adopted the name of Sharp. Catharine died in 1839.

Around the turn of the century, Charles enlarged Horton Hall considerably, although it is arguable that he added nothing to its charm. The east wing of the Revd. Thomas Sharp's house was demolished and a large, square "modern" building erected, with angular bay windows on its new Little Horton Lane frontage. A lodge stood beside the main entrance in Little Horton Lane, almost opposite the junction with Park Lane. A carriage road curved round past various outbuildings to enter the courtyard between the stables, opposite the main entrance to Thomas Sharp's house, which had now lost its pleasing symmetry. Drives also ran past the front of the new wing round to a massive, pillared entrance porch at its south west corner. This opened into a staircase hall over fifty feet long. Although two storeys high, like the earlier house, the new wing totally overshadowed the old. The old housebody, east of the tower porch now ended abruptly at a high, plain wall which rose to a shallow gable higher even than Abraham's tower. The building was of large, rectangular ashlar blocks, the clean lines having a somewhat cold and forbidding appearance compared with the charm and intimacy of the older part.

Staircase in the New Wing
(Photo Edwin Mitchell)

The house was to be a fitting "gentleman's residence" for the wealthy barrister. In the new part was a dining room approximately 32 by 20 feet, and an even larger drawing room with its bay of three long windows, each subdivided by wooden frames into small rectangular panes in the new Georgian style. Both rooms featured handsome marble chimney pieces and the dining room had two mahogany sideboards. There was a further large room north of the drawing room, the back part of it still making use of earlier walls. A doorway from this section bore the Sharp arms and led to a small room with archways at each end. The arches were partly walled up to allow normal sized doors to be inserted, but must have originally formed a passageway from the east side of the courtyard out into the park.

The grounds included a paddock and plantation as well as more formal gardens close to the house. Buildings round the courtyard provided a fuel store, wash house, coach house and stabling for eight horses. A nineteenth century gentleman's residence was not the close knit, self sufficient community of 200 years before, but a range of hen huts and pig sties testify to at least a remnant of the Hall's agricultural past.

Charles Swaine Booth Sharp did not enjoy his new home and status for long, dying childless in 1805. The considerable property that had come together during his lifetime was now re-divided. After some specific legacies, that which had come from the Swaines and the Booths was left to Charles's widowed sisters, Beatrix and Sarah, and after them to a nephew, Revd. Geoffrey Wright of Hooton Pagnall and his heirs. Hannah Gilpin Sharp, known as Madam Sharp, remained in possession of Horton Hall and a great deal of land and property in Horton and further afield. She continued to live in the Hall until her death in May 1823. After her, even the most tenuous family loyalty to Horton was lost. William Cudworth sets out the complex pattern of inheritance:

"Madam Sharp bequeathed the mansion at Horton, with all her estates in Bradford and elsewhere, to her nephew, Captain Thomas Gilpin, and his male heirs, and in default of issue to her niece, Ann Kitchen, widow of Major Kitchen, in the service of the East India Company, and her heirs; and in default to the daughters of Captain Gilpin, conditionally upon their residing at Horton. Captain Gilpin, after enjoying the estates for three years only, died at Madeira in 1826 without having married, whereupon Ann Kitchen came to the property, and married in 1828 Mr. Edward Giles, a clerk in Somerset House, for her second husband, who died in 1832, leaving an infant son, Edmund, heir to the Horton estates."

Mrs. Giles, having no need of such a large house in Yorkshire, let the greater part of it. She kept a small portion of it for her own use and lived there for a short time every year. Joshua Smith, an old servant of Madam Sharp's, was kept on as caretaker and had his own apartment consisting of an entrance hall, sitting room and kitchen and three bedrooms.

Chapter 7
John Wood and the Ten Hours Bill

Mrs. Giles' first tenant was a most distinguished Bradfordian, Mr. John Wood who had built up a small spinning business in Goodman's End between Bridge Street and Bowling Beck, until he was the largest worsted spinner in Bradford. His premises covered seven acres and employed 3,000 workers. In 1825, he and fellow mill owner John Rand had helped to settle a serious strike of woolcombers and weavers. John Wood was one of the most enlightened and humane employers in the town but even in his mill, children were working 12 or 13 hours a day.

In 1830, Wood was visited at Horton Hall by a friend, like him a member of the Church of England and the Tory party. This guest has left his name in history for the cause he was persuaded to adopt by John Wood before that visit ended. He was Richard Oastler, a land steward at Fixby and Calverley and a prominent supporter of the campaign against slavery. "You are very enthusiastic against slavery in the West Indies," said Wood, "and I assure you there are cruelties daily practised in our mills on little children, which if you knew, I am sure you would strive to prevent."

John Wood

Before Oastler left early next morning, he went to Wood's room where he found his host with a Bible in his hand. "I have had no sleep tonight," Wood told him, "I have been reading this Book and in every page I have read my own condemnation. I cannot allow you to leave me without a pledge that you will use all your influence in trying to remove from our factory system the cruelties which are practised in our mills."

Richard Oastler gave his solemn promise.

Oastler was the great activist and orator and is deservedly remembered for the Ten Hours Bill but John Wood can fairly be called the father of the agitation for factory reform. He financed the Short Time Committees and their parliamentary champion Michael Sadler. There was a huge rally in the Exchange Buildings two days after Christmas 1831 in support of the Bill. John Rand, who had not been convinced, became a firm supporter, as were two of Bradford's leading exponents of social medicine, Dr. William McTurk and Mr. William Sharp the surgeon. George Stringer Bull, Curate of Bierley, was at the meeting and became a leader of the Factory Movement. As well as financing the campaign, John Wood worked at Westminster, canvassing for Michael Sadler.

Wood's own mill was clean, and working conditions relatively good. Mr. Sharp made a weekly medical inspection. Some beatings took place, despite the mill owner's known opposition, but Wood's preferred method of discipline was to reward good work or behaviour with small bonuses and to make badly behaved children carry a card stating their fault. A visitor from the comprehensively named Society for the Diffusion of Useful Knowledge reported that Wood's sorters and combers were decent people, showing a lack of vice and drunkenness, and on good terms with their master.

In 1832, John Wood's father died, leaving over £500,000. That year, in October, John Wood opened a school for his factory children and others, one of the first 'factory schools' in England. About a thousand people attended the opening and heard how extra employees had been taken on so that

Statue of Richard Oastler, Northgate, Bradford
(Photo: J. Hansen)

500 children could leave their machines and attend school. Knitting and sewing were taught as well as reading and writing, for Wood realised that girls employed in mills from an early age would have little opportunity to acquire domestic skills needed as future wives and mothers. For fourteen years, the schoolmaster was Matthew Balme, himself to become a leading Tory factory reformer.

The Act eventually passed in 1833 made a difference of only about ten minutes a day to Wood's workers, for he had introduced the ten hour day without waiting for an Act of Parliament, and had done so without reducing wages. In November of 1833, he changed the starting time for children from 6am to 8am. Parents held a public meeting to thank him and to call for other masters to follow his example.

John Wood's first wife had died in 1828, and in 1832 he began courting Annis Elizabeth Hardy, daughter of John Hardy, who, with Wood's help on the hustings, became one of Bradford's first two Members of Parliament. (The other was Ellis Cunliffe Lister).

John and Annis were married in 1833, and the following year the mill overseers asked parents to allow their children to sing carols and present an address to Mr. Wood at Horton Hall before attending Mr. Bull's Christmas Service at Bierley Chapel. What an amazing glimpse of an unimaginably different lifestyle this must have been for those children.

Improvements in working conditions and a factory school were not John Wood's only gifts to Bradford. On October 31st 1836 he laid the foundation stone of St. James' Church in Bowling Lane (Manchester Road). Mr. Wood financed the building of this church, its schools and vicarage and provided it with an annual endowment of £350. George Bull was given the incumbency and built up an active church life. The donor's intention, supported by the Bishop of Ripon and the Vicar of Bradford, the Revd. Henry Heap, was for St. James' to become an autonomous parish. Unfortunately the next Vicar of Bradford, Revd. Dr. W. Scoresby, objected to the loss of fees to the parish church and his generally difficult attitude led to Mr. Bull moving to Birmingham and the church being closed for some years. Its parish status was eventually granted and lasted until 1965 when demographic changes led to its closure. The parish was then merged with Horton All Saints, a church not yet in existence in Mr. Wood's time.

In 1835, Mr. Wood took as a partner his half cousin, William Walker who became the managing partner of "Wood and Walker". At this time, John Wood began to sever his connections with Bradford, holding an auction of furniture from Horton Hall, and in 1840, he finally left to move to an estate at Alton in Hampshire.

Little is known of the private life of this modest man, who destroyed many of his personal papers, but an article in the Bradford Textile Society Journal quotes a tribute by John Clark, one of Wood's workmen, in 1840 : "Mr. Wood is about five feet ten inches high, has black hair, pleasant and cheerful appearance and altogether the look of the gentleman. He has had issue two daughters by his present wife. My father was in his employ fifteen years. In his sickness he visited him and paid the greatest attention toward him, and said this to the honour of my father after his visit, "that him and his house did honour to his works."

Mr. Wood and I have been on the most friendly terms. I have visited and dined with him several times. He has made me presents of money and books. I esteem the present as a great prize, not from the value but on account of the noble Donor. Throughout his life, up to the present time, he has always been characterised and distinguished for benevolence, piety and usefulness. May his life be long spared, his imitators many, his troubles few, his pleasures great, his path smooth and his death happy when called away. Mr. Wood is worth more than a Million of money."

The editor of the Journal comments that few masters earned such eulogies from working men in 1840.

Even allowing for a certain amount of hyperbole, it is clear that John Wood was a worthy successor in Christian duty and charity to the best traditions of the Sharps as master of Horton Hall.

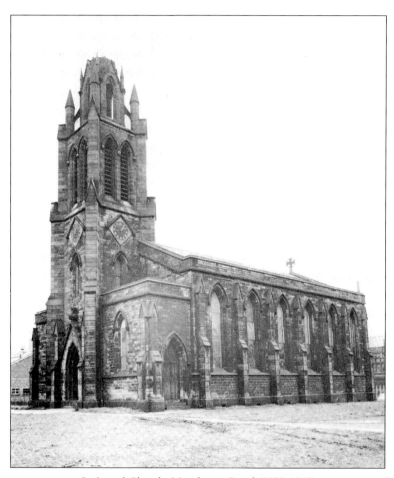

St. James' Church, Manchester Road (1838-1965)

Chapter 8
Samuel Hailstone and William Sharp

The next tenant of Horton Hall was Mr. Samuel Hailstone, who came to Bradford from York in 1783 and was articled to the Bradford solicitor John Hardy, father of the John Hardy who became one of Bradford's first Members of Parliament.

Samuel was a lively and attractive young man with dark eyes and black, curly hair. He was also energetic and outspoken, ready to voice his opinions regardless of consequence. At one time he became embroiled in a pamphlet war with another of Bradford's up and coming young men, Dr. George Mossman. Each accused the other of republican views and Samuel even threw doubt on Dr. Mossman's qualifications. The dispute came to law, but was settled out of court, thanks to intervening mediation by friends of both parties.

Samuel was a Whig, but hardly even a theoretical revolutionary. He joined the Bradford Volunteer Corps and served for ten years, rising to the rank of Major. This was a force formed in the light of growing unease about events in France, which were leading to stirrings among some of the underprivileged in England. With his dark eyes and black curls, Samuel must have been a dashing figure in his uniform of scarlet coat, turned up with buff, white breeches and leggings and black cap Their buttons were inscribed "Ready and Steady", leading to the nickname "the Rough and Readies". Fortunately the full horrors of the French Revolution did not cross the channel, there was no invasion and the only action the Volunteers saw consisted of quelling small riots and dealing with local emergencies. They acquitted themselves particularly well when they put out a potentially devastating mill fire, thought to have been started in protest at the introduction of steam engines.

Samuel eventually succeeded to John Hardy's legal practice and to his role as Law Clerk to the Leeds and Liverpool Canal. He became a large shareholder in this concern, buying when shares were available at a discount. His expectation that it would become a highly profitable concern was fully justified. (Shares which had cost Samuel Hailstone £88 each were being quoted at over £400 at the time of the death of his son Edward in 1872). He made a wise investment in the Low Moor Iron Company and also built up a large, high class legal practice.

Samuel's brother John became Woodwardian Professor of Geology at Cambridge in 1788, and played a large part in establishing the infant science of geology. Samuel too was an enthusiastic geologist, an antiquarian, and a botanist of such standing that he was elected as a Fellow of the Linnaen Society.

As his fortunes increased, Mr. Hailstone made a number of house moves, from his first Bradford home in Westgate to a small house in Great Horton Road, at which, for the furtherance of his botanical studies, he built the first greenhouse to be seen in Bradford. In 1801 he bought Croft House. He greatly enlarged this house, which stood in pleasant, wooded grounds extending from Wakefield Road to Manchester Road. The long garden, lovingly developed with a great variety of plants, was separated from the orchard by Bowling Beck.

Samuel was active in Bradford life, as well as his own business interests. He was one of the band of leading citizens who secured an Act of Parliament enabling a Board of

Dr William Sharp who married Ann Hailstone (photo courtesy of Warwicks. County Council Library, Rugby)

Commissioners to be set up to effect public watching and lighting, for the better safety of the inhabitants of the growing town. A regular watch during the dark months was instituted.

In 1808 Samuel married Ann Jones, daughter of a Bradford surgeon, and Croft House soon echoed with the sound of children. Elizabeth was born in 1809, John in 1810, Ann in 1811 and Samuel junior in 1812. Two younger boys, Thomas and William followed in 1814 and 1815, but tragedy struck in the next year when both babies died in the space of a week. Edward was born in 1818 and the last child, Frances, in 1820. Only four years later Frances died and, like the little brothers she never knew, was buried in the parish church. Sorrow came to the family again when Elizabeth died at the age of 23. Perhaps loss of two dearly loved daughters was a reason for Samuel's implacable opposition to his second daughter's marriage. Her suitor was William Sharp, surgeon, nephew to that William Sharp of Gildersome (1769-1833) who was a surgeon at St. Batholomew's Hospital, London before his appointment as Surgeon of Bradford.

William Sharp junior was born in 1805, the son of Richard Sharp, a drysalter of Gildersome. William was educated at Wakefield Grammar School and Westminster School. His Uncle Samuel was Vicar of Wakefield and William was intended for the Church. However his Uncle William took him under his wing, encouraged his medical studies on the Continent, and took him on as his assistant. These Sharps were of a branch of the Horton family, claiming both astronomer and archbishop among their kin. Although the line is not completely documented, the Sharps of Gildersome and Tong are thought to stem from one John Sharp of Tong who was a younger brother of Thomas the clothier of Horton. (Thomas died in 1607, John in 1619.)

Since Samuel Hailstone himself had married a surgeon's daughter, his objection to the match can hardly have been on social grounds, unless of course he hoped for even greater advancement for his child. Both Sharps, uncle and nephew, had attended the Hailstone family and were well known to them. Ann was lame, and delicate, so perhaps, like Patrick Bronte, his apparent selfishness was rooted in fears for his daughter's health. Whatever the reason, the couple were married by licence in Bradford Parish Church in June 1833 without her father's consent. He never spoke to her again, and if his fear had been for her health, it was soon justified, for she died in childbirth in 1834, leaving a daughter, Anne.

After his wife's death, William Sharp disposed of his practice and his house in Manor Row and went to Hull. Four years later he moved to Rugby, calling his house there Horton House, an indication perhaps of pride in his Yorkshire forebears. He had married again while at Hull, and his obituary in the Bradford Observer states that the move to Rugby was in order to place his sons under the care of Dr.A.C.Tait, Master of Rugby

School, later to be Archbishop of Canterbury. The only drawback to the school was that no Natural Science was taught. Dr. Tait agreed to make this addition to the curriculum if Dr. Sharp would become his first science teacher. Dr. Tait sent a circular to parents asking whether they would wish their sons to join a Natural Philosophy class. Dr. Sharp was appointed as Reader in Natural Philosophy and teaching began in January 1849 with a class of twenty boys. The first subject was Chemistry, illustrated with apparatus supplied by their teacher. In the second half year, the class doubled and the subject studied was Heat. In 1850 there was a change of headmaster, but Dr. Sharp's appointment was confirmed. Assured that Natural Science would continue to be taught, Dr. Sharp resigned at the end of the year to concentrate on his own profession. He had been the first ever teacher of Natural Science in a public school and from this time, science continued to be taught at Rugby, followed by other public schools.

A worthy descendant of the Sharps of Horton, William certainly shared their wide ranging enthusiasm for learning, combining, like others of his line, Christian faith and the pursuit of scientific disciplines. He wrote a book, "Practical Observations on Injuries to the Head", and many popular medical pamphlets, including papers on homeopathic medicine, of which he became a practitioner. At the age of 80, he learned Hebrew in order to read the Bible in that language. He died in 1896 at the age of 91. His obituary in the Rugby School magazine, after outlining his career, ends:

"Dr. Sharp was a very remarkable man in many ways; his medical practice was very large and successful, his interest in the progress of medical science unceasing, his zeal for sound and earnest study of the Bible unbounded, his circle of friends devoted to him. Some few years ago he retired from practice, and then devoted himself to the study of Hebrew, carrying into the investigations of Bible words the same accurate and scientific methods which he had previously applied to Therapeutics. He lived to an extreme old age, and though his sight had gone for some time, his mind was as clear and vigorous as ever. Possessing a retentive memory fully stocked with knowledge of the Hebrew Bible, he pursued his studies, with the help of friends, to the very last, and at length passed gently away, leaving behind him the memory of a life constantly devoted to accurate investigation, singularly gentle and simple and loveable."

By 1834 Samuel Hailstone was alone in Croft House. All the women of his family were dead, his wife having died in the previous year, just six months after their daughter's unwelcome marriage. Of the three surviving boys, John was at Cambridge, Samuel junior in Eastbourne for his health and Edward still at school. He, like his older brothers, went to the Grammar School at Richmond (Yorkshire). Perhaps the house held too many painful memories. It was also becoming encircled by the growing town, and in 1837 Mr. Hailstone seized the opportunity of selling the whole of the grounds as building land. Croft House itself was demolished after Croft Street was built.

Mr. Hailstone was by this time a leading authority on Yorkshire history and flora. He it was who supplied Dr. T.D. Whitaker with information on the flora of the Craven district for that gentleman's History of Craven. He had amassed an enormous library, as well as botanical and geological collections. If he was to leave Croft House, he needed to find another spacious home with a large garden. Instead of buying again, he took over the lease of Horton Hall from John Wood.

As John Wood had sold his furniture in 1835, it seems likely that Mrs. Wood and their daughter had already moved to the new home in Hampshire. Mr. Wood's continued presence in Bradford up to 1840 must have been connected with his business and the problems with St. James' Church.

The "new" wing of the hall became Mr. Hailstone's living quarters. It provided spacious reception rooms and three large bedrooms, as well as a range of kitchens, pantries and larders described as being in a sort of annex along a wide stone passage. Some of these service facilities had been created by subdividing Charles Swain Booth Sharp's third large room, to the north of the drawing room, others occupied the rest of the run of buildings on the east side of the courtyard. A large lawn sloped down from the drawing room windows and there was abundant space for greenhouses, parterres and herbaceous borders. The older part of the house, romantically mantled with ivy and creepers, was given over to the ever growing library and collections, except for rooms still reserved for Mrs. Giles. While at the Hall, Samuel Hailstone established a collection of antiquities which included many relics and manuscripts concerning Abraham Sharp, and other items on which John James was able to draw when producing his History of Bradford. The museum of geological specimens was described as unique in its day.

As well as the sad series of family losses, Samuel was without a partner in his legal practice, following the death of Mr. John Thompson when the Rothsay Castle was wrecked in the Menai Straits in 1831. However, Edward was on the point of leaving school, and returned to Bradford to live with his father and become his pupil. Samuel junior also came to live at Horton Hall, where he predeceased his father.

Samuel Hailstone senior died at Horton Hall in 1851, at the age of 84, having become a much respected figure in Bradford, both as lawyer and citizen. Of his eight children, he left two surviving sons. John, the elder, was a clergyman with a Master of Arts degree from Trinity College, Cambridge, and held the living of Bottisham, Cambridge for over thirty years.

Chapter 9
The Biggest Hailstone

Edward Hailstone stayed on in Horton Hall. An agreement dated 23rd August 1852, between Ann Giles of Tavistock Place, Tavistock Square, Middlesex, Widow; and Edward Hailstone of Horton Hall in the Parish of Bradford in the County of York, Esquire, leased to Edward:

"the house, outbuildings, gardens, fixtures and furnishings, also a paddock and plantation about three acres, lately in the occupation of Edward Hailstone and Joshua Smith, and the pews or sittings in Bradford Parish Church, for 21 years."

The terms of the lease included permission to demolish certain outbuildings at the north of Laurel Court and east of the drying yard and from the premises occupied by Joshua Smith. This had the effect of creating one large courtyard. Mr. Hailstone was also to have free use of the cottage or lodge near the Halifax road.

Various rooms and their contents are listed in the lease. The new part had the fine hall and reception rooms already described, while upstairs were the new French bedroom, or west chamber, the green room, large bedroom or octagon room, and the far white room and near white room of unspecified use. The old part contained a hall and library, which was the old dining room, with bedrooms above for housekeeper, maidservants and menservants. The old kitchen contained a large range, a smoke jack and an iron oven, a kitchen table and a deer's head with antlers! The new kitchen, by contrast had a large range with oven and boiler and a Crane cooking apparatus, a pump and a sink. There was a larder in the old part, with stone tables and seventeen beef hooks. The house was also equipped with dairy, wine cellar, brewhouse, baking oven, butler's pantry, servants' hall, laundry, boot and shoe room, and that most modern convenience, a water closet with seat and apparatus, pipes and cistern, complete.

Mrs. Giles' property in Horton was much more extensive than the immediate surroundings of the Hall, and she had already begun to dispose of some of it. An Act allowing this had been passed in 1839. Building land listed for sale at this time included the areas on both sides of Little Horton Lane, from Melbourne Place to Edmund Street, including Lansdowne place, on the west, and on the east from Ann Place to Back Road (about the present site of the skating rink). The parkland in which the Hall stood extended on both sides of Little Horton Lane, bounded on the east by Park Lane. A carriage road ran from the Hall right through to Great Horton Road, following approximately the line of the present Ashgrove, with a porter's lodge almost opposite the west end of Melbourne Place.

There were other holdings of land, barns and houses at Dirkhill, Hollingwood Lane, Paradise, Ashfield Terrace and Chesham Street off Great Horton Road, Aycliffe Lane (later called Haycliffe), Southgate and Southfield Lane. None of this property was the concern of the tenant of Horton Hall and even the fourteen acres of park on the far side of Little Horton Lane were sold for £4000 to the Bradford Union. Here the foundation stone of the new workhouse was laid in 1851. The building opened in 1852 amid much civic congratulation about its size, modernity and provision for the comfort of its inmates, an appraisal not necessarily shared by those who became its clients.

Edward Hailstone
(photo courtesy of Mr Alan and the late Mr John Hitchcock)

Edward Hailstone succeeded to his father's legal practice, but left its general work largely to his partners. His chief business interests lay with those companies for which he was Law Clerk – the Leeds and Liverpool Canal Company, the Bradford Canal Company, the Worsted Committees of Yorkshire, Lancashire and Cheshire, and several Turnpike Trusts. He was legal adviser to the Low Moor Company and Clerk to the Trustees of Bradford Grammar School. His services to the Leeds and Liverpool Canal Company were quite outstanding. His knowledge of all aspects of the Company, including the relevant Acts of Parliament, was comprehensive, and he pursued a successful policy of avoiding litigation as much as possible.

Edward also became Secretary of the St. George's Hall Company. This fine building, Messrs Lockwood and Mawson's first municipal commission, was opened in August 1853 and Edward was among those helping to entertain the distinguished guests. The Queen and Prince Albert were Patrons, but did not attend the opening. Nevertheless, there was a most distinguished gathering. The Earl and Countess of Harewood brought a large party from Harewood House, Mr. Titus Salt brought a party from Crow Nest near Halifax, Mr. Samuel Cunliffe Lister from Manningham Hall, Mr. Rowland Winn from Nostell Priory, and both Bradford's Members of Parliament, Mr. H.W.Wickham and Alderman Robert Milligan, brought parties. The Church was well represented by the Archbishop of York, the Most Revd. Thomas Musgrave and the Hon. Mrs. Musgrave, the Bishop of Ripon, the Right Revd. Charles Longley and the Hon. Mrs. Longley, the Archdeacon of Craven, the Venerable Charles Musgrave and Mrs. Musgrave, and the Vicar of Bradford the Revd. Dr.John Burnet.

Like the Hailstones, the Archbishop and his elder brother, the Archdeacon, were both old boys of Richmond Grammar School and the Archbishop had held the Trinity College living of Bottisham, later held by John Hailstone.

The opening concert began with the National Anthem with Madame Clara Novello as soloist, followed by a performance of Mendelssohn's oratorio St. Paul. Afterwards the Harewood party were entertained by the Mayor, Alderman Samuel Smith, who had been the driving force behind the whole project. The Church party were Edward Hailstone's guests at Horton Hall. Edward's brother John and his wife Jane stayed at Horton Hall for the occasion, which took the form of three days of musical performances. Jane wrote in her diary:

"After the concert we entertained the Archbishop of York and his lady, the Bishop of Ripon, Dr. Longley, and his lady, Archdeacon Musgrave and numerous others, to lunch at Horton, a cold dinner at five, then dressed for the evening concert." She recorded the evening concert as miscellaneous and rather tedious. Thursday brought Handel's Messiah, another large party to lunch and another miscellaneous concert. Friday morning had Haydn's Creation, which charmed Jane, followed by Israel in Egypt, which she liked less, it being almost all chorus. The evening saw a return to Mendelssohn with A Midsummer Night's Dream.

How splendid these gatherings at Horton Hall must have been, the fine mahogany sideboards laden, the table set with silver and crystal. Sartorially, the distinguished clergy might well have outshone their ladies, particularly in their evening attire of breeches and silk stockings, with a short cassock of rich purple or black ribbed silk, topped by a frogged dress coat. Their host himself would not have lagged behind. A contemporary account

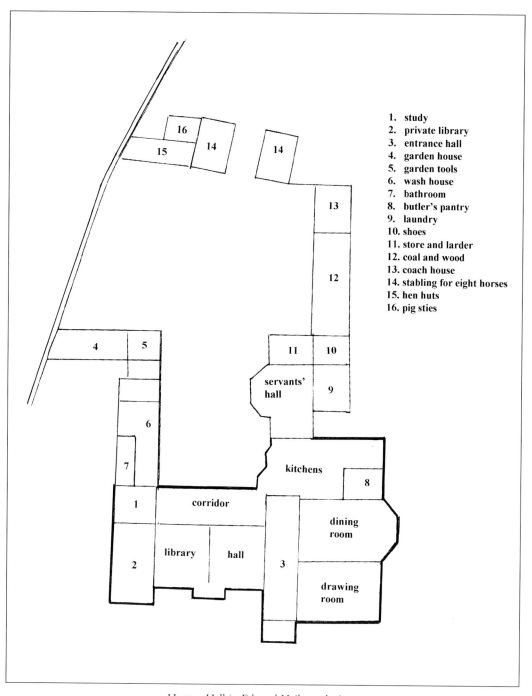

Horton Hall in Edward Hailstone's time.

refers to him as he, "impervious to convention, walked the streets of Bradford in a blue coat with spade guineas for buttons, while all around him were in subfusc."

Another says. "He was of massive build, tall and handsome in appearance, and when dressed in a black velvet suit with knickerbockers, low shoes and broad brimmed hat, he looked the type of an English gentleman. In the library of Horton Hall his appearance was thoroughly in harmony with the oak-panelled rooms and their associations." A photograph taken later in his life shows a most distinguished, tall and bearded gentleman clad in a quite extraordinarily loud checked plus fours suit with matching stockings.

Edward Hailstone and Alderman Samuel Smith were instrumental in founding the Bradford Festival Choral Society and many leading musicians visited Horton Hall during Bradford's music festivals in 1853 and 1856. Edward was an active member of many distinguished bodies - the Yorkshire Archaeological Society, the National Archaeological Society, the Athenaeum Club, the Geological Society, the British Association and the Social Science Congress. He was a Fellow of the Society of Antiquaries. He added very considerably to the documents and books inherited from his father, but disposed of the botanical specimens, in which he had little interest, to the Philosophical Society's Museum at York. The geological collection went to Leicester.

His ability was recognised far more widely than in his native town when the Prince Consort sought his advice when planning the Great Exhibition. His commission reads:

"Society of Arts and Commerce, London.

Edward Hailstone Esq., of Horton Hall, is authorised by His Royal Highness Prince Albert, as President of the Society of Arts and Commerce, to ascertain the views and opinions with reference to the expediency of forming a great Industrial Exhibition, to be held in London in the year 1851.

Albert.

Osborne House, October 5th 1849."

ST. GEORGE'S HALL, BRADFORD
Opened 31st August, 1853.

He received a diploma dated October 15th 1851, signed by the Prince, and a medal, for the services rendered by him to the Commissioners of the Exhibition.

The perspicacious Jane Austen opened one of her best known works with the statement that:

"It is a truth universally acknowledged that a single man in possession of a good fortune must be in want of a wife."

When the man has not only a good fortune, but good intellect, good looks and good social connections, it seems quite remarkable that he should have reached the age of 37 and still be a bachelor. When Hailstone did marry, in 1855, it was as spectacular as the rest of his life. His chosen bride was Sarah Harriette Lilla, only daughter of William Busfeild Ferrand of St. Ives and Harden Grange, Bingley. Miss Ferrand had been a ward in Chancery, living under her father's guardianship until 1853, after which, she went to live with her uncle, Edward Hailstone's close friend Mr. J.A. Busfeild, at Upwood, Bingley.

Stained Glass Window commemorating Edward Hailstone's Marriage. Now in the Old Turk's Head Public House, Dewsbury. (Photo: J. Hansen)

Mr. Ferrand, who was only nine years older than the bridegroom, neither approved nor consented, but was powerless to prevent the match.

A Bradford journalist has left an account of the wedding:

"The marriage of our townsman Edward Hailstone Esq., was the occasion of considerable excitement in Bingley yesterday. From an early hour the streets had an unusually busy appearance, and as time wore on, it seemed as if the whole population of the town had turned out en masse. The churchyard was besieged by an excited crowd long before the time fixed for the ceremony, and numerous were the disappointed applicants for admission into the sacred edifice.

The wedding party, in a long train of carriages, arrived from Upwood at half past ten. The service was performed by the Lord Bishop of Ripon assisted by Revd. J. Cheadle, Vicar of Bingley. The bride (Miss Ferrand) was given away by her uncle, J.A. Busfeild Esq.. As the Bishop pronounced the important words "Those whom God hath joined together, let no man put asunder," a cannon on the canal banks was fired and the reverberation seemed almost to shake the church. The firing was repeated during the morning. At the close of the ceremony, as the party retired to the vestry, the Hallelujah Chorus was played on the organ and the bells struck up a merry peal."

What the bride's father thought, if he could hear all this from St. Ive's, we shall never know, but perhaps can guess!

For the first time in many years, Horton Hall again housed a nursery, when Etheldreda Lilla was born in 1858 and Wilfred Edward in 1864. In the year of his marriage, Edward was elected as Vicar's Warden of Bradford Parish Church and typically, he took a lively interest in church matters. During his time, the long planned remodelling of the interior of the building was begun, starting with the removal of the east gallery. In 1864 a magnificent new church was consecrated, almost on his doorstep, and Edward became the first Vicar's Warden of All Saints', holding this office until 1867,

The Hailstones stayed at Horton Hall until 1871, at which time they removed to Walton Hall near Wakefield, taking with them Edward's great collection of antiquities. Mrs. Hailstone had her collection too, of lace and antique needlework, on which she was an expert. The Hailstone marriage lasted longer than some contemporaries had predicted for two such strong characters, but ended in divorce in 1878. A descendant of the family suggests that squabbles over books led to the rift. Of Edward's death in 1890, the same source commented: "The biggest Hailstone ever dropped."

Chapter 10
For Sale

By the time the Hailstones left, Horton Hall was in the hands of trustees under the terms of Ann Giles' will. Mrs.Giles died in December 1854. Her son Edmund had gone to Australia the previous year, but he died only three days after arriving in Sydney. When the Hall was without tenant, the trustees put the whole of the remaining estate up for sale by auction. The last of the holdings, so shrewdly amassed over the centuries since the first Sharp yeomen emerged from the feudal system, were to be dispersed.

A large, unoccupied house, with the buildings of a growing town steadily encroaching, could easily have suffered the same fate as Croft House, but for Horton Hall, help was at hand.

In 1862, a piece of land had been purchased by Horton Hall's next door neighbour, the occupant of Horton Old Hall. This was described as "2976 square yards, bounded on the east by the intended road called Ash Grove, and on the south by Francis Sharp Powell's land, being part of the estate of the late Hannah Gilpin Sharp, lately in occupation of Samuel Hailstone." The following year, Mr. Powell purchased a further 420 square yards for the purpose of improving his land and straightening an irregular border.

In 1743, Isaac Sharp, the last male heir of the Royalist Sharps of Horton Old Hall, died, leaving a daughter, Dorothy. Dorothy married Francis Stapleton and bore him three children. Their son and hoped for heir, christened Sharp, died in infancy and the estate once again passed through the female line to their elder daughter Elizabeth. Elizabeth married Francis Bridges and they had three daughters and a son, Francis Sharp. Francis Sharp Bridges duly inherited Horton Old Hall and its estates, but never married. When he died in 1844, the estate was left to his seventeen year old great nephew, Francis Sharp Powell.

Young Francis also inherited property in Lancashire from his father, the Revd. Benjamin Powell, incumbent of St. George's Church, Wigan.

Francis Sharp Powell was educated at Wigan Grammar School, Uppingham and Sedbergh, before gaining a place at St. John's College, Cambridge as a Lupton Scholar and subsequently reading Law in London. Although called to the bar of the Inner Temple, Mr. Powell chose a political career and was at various times Conservative Member of Parliament for Wigan, Cambridge and the Northern Division of the West Riding. His married life began in 1858 in his father's house, Bellingham Lodge, in Wigan, but in 1860 he leased 1 Cambridge Square, Hyde Park. Thereafter, Francis and Annie Powell divided their time between London and Horton Old Hall.

In Horton, Francis chose the role of benevolent country squire. Although the town was expanding rapidly, he refused to sell land on Little Horton Green, or the fields around his home. Increased taxes on undeveloped land in towns actually exceeded the rent he could get from his rural enclave, but he refused to turn tenants out of their cottages to make way for so-called improvements. Sporadic coal mining had scarred the green, but Francis had the land restored to good order as well as repairing cottages, hedges and boundary walls.

The only item lacking to complete an authentic village was a church in the medieval tradition. In this direction the squire's inclination coincided perfectly with the needs of the

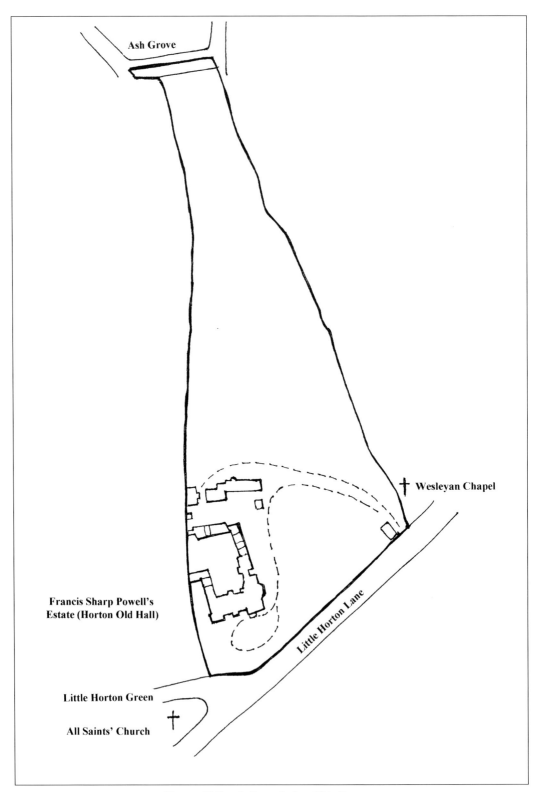

Horton Hall and Grounds, late 19th Century

Sir Francis Sharp Powell

town. The huge shifts and growths of population in the early part of the century led to a House of Lords Commission on Spiritual Destitution in 1858. A Bradford Church Building Society was formed in 1859, aiming to provide ten new churches within five years - it actually took nearer to twelve years. All Saints', consecrated in 1864, was the most splendid of them, and regarded as the finest achievement of the architects, Mallinson and Healey. Its site opposite Horton Old Hall was given, and the building totally financed, by Francis Sharp Powell who also provided a school and vicarage. He contributed land and generous donations of money for the building of more of the new churches. For his benevolence and other public spirited work, he was made a Baronet in 1892 and granted the freedom of the City of Bradford in 1902. (Bradford gained city status in 1897).

Horton Old Hall was tastefully furnished with works of art, antiques and a fine library. The Powells enjoyed a gracious and romantic lifestyle aimed at recapturing a rather idealised version of an earlier age. Gas, electricity and the telephone were forbidden, illumination provided by oil lamps. Francis Sharp Powell's nephew and biographer relates that "Every Christmas, the All Saints' choirboys sang and were regaled in good old English style in the dark panelled hall of Horton Old Hall, with its pictures and armour, high mullioned windows, oak gallery and blazing fire."

Twice a year, feasts for their tenants were held, when farmers from Powell lands as far away as Haworth came for two days of banquets. Geese, turkeys, pies, cheeses, barrels of ale and gallons of punch were provided.

The great auction of the Giles estates took place on Monday, August 7th 1871, at the Talbot Hotel in Bradford. The property for sale comprised "Horton Hall Estate together with a farm of eleven and a half acres at Great Horton and other building land in Chesham Street and Great Horton Road." The estate was offered as 37 lots.

All Saints' Church, Little Horton
(photo: J. Hansen)

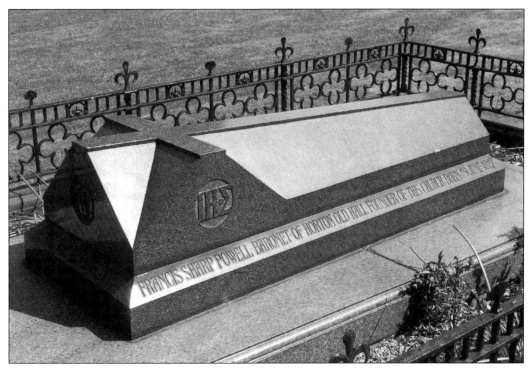
The Grave of Sir Francis Sharp Powell, All Saints' Church
(photo: J. Hansen)

Lots 1 - 19 specified individual building plots around Ashgrove and Trinity Terrace.

Lot 20 was described thus: "The mansion known as Horton Hall, lately the residence of Edward Hailstone Esq., with the stables, coach house and other out-offices, gardens and shrubberies, and containing in the whole an area of 13,814 square yards or thereabouts. The older portion of Horton Hall, with the observatory where Abraham Sharp, the celebrated mathematician, conducted his astronomical observations, will present many features of interest to the antiquarian, whilst the modern part renders it desirable for a gentleman's residence. The grounds, ornamental timbers, shrubberies etc. are all in perfect keeping, whilst the valuable and extensive frontages enhance the value for building purposes. There is also a supply of water by special service pipes." The lot was bounded by Little Horton Lane, Little Horton Green, the Horton Old Hall estate and Ashgrove Road.

Lots 21 - 36 were building land around Chesham Street, Southfield Lane and Haycliffe Lane.

Lot 37, farm, house and land at Southfield Lane.

For just over £10,000, Francis Sharp Powell purchased lots 1 - 20 including a moiety of Ashgrove where it was co-extensive with the northern boundary of his land, and a right of way along the whole of Ashgrove and Lower Ashgrove, giving access from the Hall to Great Horton Road. He undertook to pave and flag his portion of the road and maintain it in the same way that Bradford did for the rest of it.

The building lots in his purchase came with the specification that no dwelling on them should be of less annual value than £20, which meant that they were suitable for villas rather than workmen's cottages.

Ezra Waugh Hammond

Joseph Cawthra

After the death of Faith Sawrey in 1767, the ownership of Horton Hall had moved from the Sharp family, even though the name had for a time been adopted. Now it was back in the capable and loving hands of a direct descendant of its original owner. The Bradford Burgess Rolls show that from 1877 to 1885 Matthew Wright occupied the Hall, and the 1881 Census lists a housekeeper and a female servant at the Hall and a gardener with his wife and son, also a gardener, at the lodge. The Burgess and Electoral Rolls list no one between 1886 and 1890, but the house and grounds were maintained in good order, presumably by Mr. Powell's staff from Horton Old Hall.

In 1890, Mr. Powell leased Horton Hall to Alderman Ezra Waugh Hammond, Mayor of Bradford. Mr. Hammond was a most suitable tenant to take care of such a house. He had a great interest in history and a love of his native town. A descendant of a family named in the Horton Poll Tax list in 1379, he was born in 1836 at Four Lane Ends, where his father James kept the Craven Heifer public house. James Hammond later moved to the Market Tavern, and in 1860 bought the Fountain Brewery in Manchester Road. Ezra served an apprenticeship in the worsted trade, but joined the brewery business as it grew. He developed it and managed it until it was made into a limited company in 1891 as Hammonds United Breweries Ltd. He was Chairman of the Bradford Brewers' Association and the Association of Yorkshire Brewers. He had been a member of the Town Council for Little Horton Ward for nine years when he was elected Mayor in 1890. His proposer said that he believed that while Mr. Hammond wore the Mayoral chain it would receive no tarnish or diminution of lustre. His seconder said that he was a man of means, which Bradford needed. They required not only a man equal to the duty of laying foundation stones, but also of good moral character, ability, sound judgement, impartiality, a man of ambition, proud of his town and anxious for its highest development. As a definition of a civic leader, this is worthy of being carved in stone and set up in the Council Chamber. It must have been a recognisable assessment of Mr. Hammond, for he was elected unanimously.

He was described as bald and bearded, portly, genial and active. Politically he was a moderate Conservative. He was a Freemason, a governor of the Grammar School and a member of Salem Congregational Church. He was 54 years old and a widower when he moved into Horton Hall with two of his six daughters and a staff of housekeeper, cook and three maids.

There was a short gap between Mr. Hammond's occupancy and the next tenant, another who had risen by his own hard work to a position of wealth and influence. Joseph Cawthra was a native of Great Horton. At the age of thirteen he went to work for Taylor and Rumboll, Stuff Merchants. This firm collapsed while he was actually in London on business for them. Joseph set up his own concern there, and soon returned to Bradford to establish himself as a merchant in Italian cloth linings. Cawthra, Jacques and Co. became one of the leading houses with an extensive merchant and manufacturing business with branches in London, Manchester, Glasgow and Paris. Later his company became Joseph Cawthra and Co. Ltd. with a works at Dudley Hill and city centre premises at 7, 9 and 11 Swaine Street, one of the streets commemorating a former master of Horton Hall.

He married Mary Jane Briggs, daughter of a timber merchant, and they had a son, John William Briggs Cawthra. His son's death led to a most generous gift to Bradford by way of a memorial. At a cost of £10,000 Joseph Cawthra bought the land and paid for the building of St. Catherine's House in St. Mary's Road, Manningham, as a hospital for cancer and incurable diseases. He was President of Bradford Royal Infirmary, Vice-President of Bradford Textile Society and a Justice of the Peace. Mr. Cawthra died in 1908 and the Hall was again empty.

Perhaps there was now a shortage of potential tenants wanting such a large house in an area fast becoming an anachronistic oasis surrounded by the full thrust and business of an industrial city. Sir Francis Sharp Powell died in 1911 and when his estates were listed for tax purposes, Horton Hall was described as a

"messuage or dwelling house with stables, outbuildings and garden ground cottage and lodge, the messuage now being divided into two dwelling houses; one of such dwelling houses and the cottage being occupied by Mr. N.White, together with the field adjoining, as lesee for a term of five years from the 15th day of May 1911, the remaining portion of the messuage being unoccupied." Its value was given as £7000, while Horton Old Hall and its grounds, where Lady Powell continued to live, were valued at £2500.

The Electoral Roll for 1913-14 lists Norman Arthur White at Horton Hall and in 1918 it is occupied by Mr. and Mrs. Albert Norman White.

An idea of Sir Francis Sharp Powell's impact on the social, philanthropic, political and business life of the city can be deduced from the total value of his Bradford estates, excluding his property in Lancashire and London. An estate of £309,396 included Crossley Hall, Allerton Hall, Bents Farm and the Ling Bob Public House and cottages at Wilsden, the Duke of York Beer House, and property at Bingley, Cullingworth, Oxenhope, Haworth, Bramley, Gildersome, Wortley and Heckmondwike.

Chapter 11
Not Quite a Palace

Bradford had achieved phenomenal growth during the previous century, both in population and prosperity. One outcome of this growth had been the conferring of city status in 1897. During this same growth period, the hierarchy of the Church of England was realising that the ancient dioceses into which the country was divided were becoming inappropriate and unworkable. In 1836 the Diocese of Ripon had been formed out of parts of the vast older Dioceses of Chester and York. Its first bishop was that Dr. Longley who was Edward Hailstone's guest at the opening of St. George's Hall. By the early years of the twentieth century there was a growing movement for further subdivision. The first World War brought a temporary halt to such considerations, but in November 1919 the Order in Council was signed, bringing the new Diocese of Bradford into being. This covered an area of 880 square miles with a population of 600,000. It stretched from just north of Sedbergh to the southern edge of Bradford, from Bentham in the west to Leathley in the east. There were several contenders for Cathedral of the new diocese, including Holy Trinity Church, Skipton. This would have been more central to the area, but not to the density of population. Some thought that Francis Sharp Powell's beautiful, soaring All Saints' might have been chosen, but in the end the decision was the obvious one of Bradford's ancient Parish Church of St. Peter.

Bradford now also required a suitable home for a bishop. The Registrar and chief mentor of the new diocese was Bradford solicitor F. A. T. Mossman, great grandson of that Dr. George Mossman whose early relationship with Samuel Hailstone had been so stormy. Fortunately their duels had been conducted with words rather than swords, or local history might have turned out quite differently. Mr. Mossman and the other members of the Bishopric Committee were determined that this was to be a modern bishopric. They wanted a clear distinction drawn between a modest income for the bishop and the necessary expenses of the office, although they were unable to get this written into the constitution. They were also adamant that there should be no palace, but a suitable but not excessive house. Finding this proved a real headache. Many properties were inspected and rejected on grounds of location or some unsuitable feature. Lady Powell had offered Horton Hall at an early stage. A letter from her solicitors in 1917 made an offer "on behalf of Lady Powell and Mr. Francis Sharp Bardsley, the tenant for life and tenant in tail respectively of the Yorkshire estates of the late Sir Francis Sharp Powell, of Horton Hall as a residence for the bishop, on a repairing lease for 21 years at a nominal rent of £10 per annum."

The committee really hoped to purchase a house, but eventually, when Lady Powell had agreed to some alterations, they took up her offer, intending it to be a temporary measure.

An article in the Yorkshire Observer Budget, 9th August 1919, by Isabel Rayfield describes the hall while still occupied by Mr. and Mrs. Norman White: "...much of the older hall of the 14th century remains, the newer building encasing the old. The room at the back shows evidence of the greatest antiquity, the carved plaster ceiling being 14th century, also the panelling. A fine old door leads from here to the courtyard. Rooms to the front are loftier with fine ingle fireplaces and large mullioned windows. The modern portion of the hall was added at the end of the 17th century by another member of the family and seems quite out of keeping with the charm of the old hall with which it is connected." The writer goes on to refer to: "memories of the Sharps, this family of whom Bradford should be so justly proud, and it is the greatest pleasure to find the fine old mansion so perfectly kept and appreciated. Many of the massive oak dressers or sideboards are unique, the carved four-poster bedsteads are enhanced by almost regal draperies, candlesticks and snuffers stand just where they should, and flowers adorn all the rooms, a foil to the dark woodwork, while pewter, old china and pictures cause one to linger continually."

The journalist is mistaken by a century, or misprinted, regarding the date of the 'modern' addition, but her description of the house in 1919 is interesting, and shows how Mr. and Mrs. White cared for it and sought out appropriate furnishings.

As well as the plaster work in the oldest part, the main room of the Jacobean house, west of the entrance porch, had some very fine work indeed. There was a frieze with columns flanking panels of swags, urns, cherubs' heads and tendrils and the ceiling was divided into square compartments by beams, the compartments being decorated with plaster in two alternate designs. One consisted of the Sharp arms and crest within an elaborate chaplet, or wreath, with cherubs' heads in the spandrels; the other had moulded diagonal ribs to a central lozenge decorated with a heraldic badge of a fox bearing in its mouth a Maltese Cross fitchy (its arms ending in points).

This then was the house to which the Right Revd. Arthur Perowne brought his wife, Helena Frances, and the youngest of his three sons in 1920. The middle, bay-windowed room on the first floor of the new wing, above the Georgian drawing room, was made into a simple chapel. Horton Hall once again housed a room licensed for worship, this time for the Established Church.

Arthur William Thomson Perowne was an excellent choice as the first Bishop of Bradford. The Perownes are a family of Huguenot descent and have provided many distinguished churchmen. The new bishop's father had been Bishop of Worcester and Arthur had for a time been his chaplain. He was Vicar of St. George's Church, Edgbaston at the time when the new Diocese of Birmingham was formed out of the old Diocese of Worcester, and immediately before coming to Bradford was Archdeacon of Plymouth. All this experience stood him in good stead in the formative years of Bradford Diocese. He was an efficient administrator and particularly keen to establish good financial order. At the same time, deep spiritual commitment was the driving force behind all his actions. When his appointment was announced, the Telegraph and Argus responded to curiosity about the new bishop with a description:

"The Bishop is of medium height and slight build. He is clean shaven, has abundant grey hair and has finely-cut features. The nose is straight, and the mouth, one imagines, might on occasion be very straight; but there are many humorous wrinkles about the eyes, and the corners of the mouth are quick to turn up in a smile."

The bishop was enthroned by the Bishop of Ripon in what was now Bradford Cathedral in February 1920. So here was one tenant of Horton Hall who had no need of the pew in the parish church which came with the lease! In fact pew rents were almost immediately abolished and all seats in the cathedral were free from Easter Sunday, 1920.

Bishop Perowne (right) with Bishop Stanton Jones (formerly Vicar of Bradford) at Horton Hall 1930

Dr. Perowne came with a reputation for deep concern for social welfare and a willingness to work closely with the Nonconformist Churches on such issues. He pointed out in his enthronement sermon that the new diocese was beginning its life at a critical period of national history. We were suffering from disillusionment, disappointment, industrial troubles, financial instability, reckless extravagance, a wave of crime, a mad rush after pleasure and a superstitious craving for contact with the unseen. These were issues with which the Church of Christ was called upon to grapple. He explained, however, that the bettering of social conditions was not his primary concern. "No one", he said, "is keener than I on social reform, but the religion of Christ must permeate the whole of life." He outlined what he saw as the roles of clergy, laity and bishops to this end.

Politically, the new bishop believed that the Church and the new and growing Labour Party must get to know each other better, but he was not personally committed to any party, preferring to make a considered judgement on each issue and vote according to his conscience. So successfully did he do this that after a by-election in Plymouth, all three candidates claimed to have had his support!

Horton Hall was not quite ready for their occupancy and the family lived at first in White Lodge in Heaton, by arrangement with its owner, Mr. Thomas Howarth, who was abroad for a time. They moved into the hall in April and spoke about their new home at a reception given by the Mayor of Pudsey. Mrs. Perowne said how much they were looking forward to inviting people. They did not intend to give grand entertainments, but hoped they would in time see everyone present at Horton Hall. She hoped that the hall would become an "open house" for diocesan work. The Bishop confided that he mowed his own lawn and laid his own stair carpet - far from the remote and grand image of some bishops of previous generations.

Many years later, Leslie Perowne, the bishop's youngest son, recalled their days at the hall. Coming from Plymouth, between the sea and the moors and wild spaces of Devon, his first impression was of the blackness of Bradford. From the chapel window he could look out over what seemed to him a hundred belching mill chimneys. As a boy of 14, he chose to sleep outdoors one summer night, only to awake next morning covered in black smuts. He remembered the big rooms of the Georgian wing being ideal for entertaining and various meetings. He remembered some staffing difficulties too. Since the war, positions in domestic service were getting harder to fill and although the Perownes had a maid when they first came, there was a spell after she left when there was a rota (which included the bishop) for domestic chores, including getting up early to light the fires. Leslie remembered a maid who played the violin in her bedroom, and smoked, and later a man servant who got drunk.

In 1922 a mission campaign team of undergraduates came to Bradford from Cambridge University. It was organised by the bishop's second son, Stewart, and Horton Hall became campaign headquarters. Stewart later became a distinguished Orientalist, Historian and Colonial Administrator. The eldest son, Francis, worked for the Bank of London and South America in Paraguay and Argentina. It was during what should have been a joyful time for family members working together in mission, that their faith was tested by a great sorrow. Early in the morning of September 22nd, Mrs. Perowne died. She had been seriously ill for some time and had a major operation a year previously, but until the last few days, ill health had not stopped her activity and interest in a wide range of diocesan and national

Church organisations. One of the many obituaries published sums up the impression she had made in her short time in Bradford:

"The news of the death of Mrs. Perowne will be a great blow to the diocese. Since coming to Bradford she has actively associated herself with the work of the Bishopric, and her help in the Mothers' Union, the Girls' Friendly Society, and in many other activities will long be remembered. It was always a delight to listen to her addresses – they were given in such a homely, natural way, so full of sympathy and the human touch. She had a big loving heart, and possessed a keen sense of humour, and wherever she went readily made friends." There is a beautiful memorial window in the south transept of Bradford Cathedral.

After Mrs. Perowne's death, an elderly cousin, Laura Barradale, moved in to take charge of the housekeeping. In 1926, Bishop Perowne married again. Mabel Bailey had been a Sunday School teacher at St. George's Church, Edgbaston, when Arthur Perowne was vicar there. She had gone to India with the Church Missionary Society and become Principal of a school at Nasik. After Mrs. Perowne's death, Mabel and Arthur had corresponded and in 1925 she came home. As bishop's wife, she continued her interest in the work of the Church overseas and helped to develop support in the diocese for missionary organisations.

Bishop Perowne stayed in Bradford for eleven years, and the circumstances of his going were unusual. The Bishopric of Worcester was vacant following the death of the Right Revd. E. H. Pearce. The position was offered to Canon A.W.F.Blunt, Vicar of St. Werburgh's, Derby. He accepted, but stunned Worcester diocesan officials by declaring that one of his first actions would be to dispose of Hartlebury Castle, in which he was not prepared to live. "Sooner or later," he said, "the diocese will have to face the question of selling the house or adapting it for other diocesan purposes besides episcopal residence. I should invite them to grasp the nettle at once. In doing this, I should feel I was conferring a real service on the diocese."

Although the movement for housing bishops more modestly was growing, Worcester was not quite ready for such a drastic step. This left Prime Minister Ramsay MacDonald with a double dilemma – to find a different bishop for Worcester and to find a bishopric for Canon Blunt, whom he was convinced would be a refreshing asset to the Bench of Bishops. Arthur Perowne was a man who had already lived in Hartlebury Castle when his father was Bishop of Worcester. He was also a man with a strong sense of duty and obligation and when the offer of Worcester was made, he accepted. He was sorry to leave Bradford and no exponent of grand living, but he said that if it was felt to be indispensable that the bishop should live in Hartlebury, until some other plans could be made for the use of the house, it was the duty of the bishop to go there.

The Leeds Mercury of January 24th 1931 carried this interview by reporter Joe Illingworth:

"The Bishop of Bradford stared wistfully out of the windows of his library at Horton Hall this evening and remarked:- 'One of the things we regret as much as anything is leaving the old Hall. The moment you enter the courtyard everything is at once so unexpectedly quiet, quaint and old-world. I cannot imagine any place which has lent itself more completely to a Bishop's house than this has. It is so comfortable, so homely. When we returned from a visit to Hartlebury Castle last week, I remarked to my wife on the homely cosiness that is here.'

He told me it is probable he will continue to live at Horton Hall until the very day before his enthronement at Worcester, which he will endeavour to arrange for about the last Saturday in March.

'It is going to be a tremendously hard thing for me to leave Bradford because I have made so many friends. The roots have gone deep.'"

Arthur Perowne was regarded in Bradford with respect and affection for his broad views, sincerity, kindness and charitable nature. He related well to Bradford's wool men, though John Peart-Binns, writing in 1969 commented that he seemed unable to stand up to them and when they needed a bracing tonic he offered soothing syrup. The Yorkshire Post however, in 1931, recorded that he would be long remembered as one of the few men outside the woollen industry who strove ceaselessly to avert the costly wages dispute and stoppage of the previous year.

No sooner had Bishop Perowne accepted Worcester than Bradford was offered to Canon Blunt. His appointment was announced in February 1931, but a succession of illnesses delayed his enthronement until November. A detailed account of the formation of the diocese and the lives and work of its successive bishops can be found in the author's "One Small Corner - a History of Bradford Diocese."

Chapter 12
Blunt

Bradford and Blunt were made for each other. The diocese's acres of rural beauty, often concealing rural poverty, coupled with the social concerns and industrial problems of the city, were meat and drink to this outspoken, reforming churchman. The diocesan policy of no palace suited him, and the city that gave birth to the Independent Labour Party accorded well with his well known political views. However, for Margaret and Alfred Blunt's four children, the best things about the move were the prospect of a motor car and a house with electric light. Nineteen year old Amy was asked by a reporter if she had heard the rumour that the hall was haunted, but dismissed it robustly as "Absolute rubbish. I have never been in a house which seems less likely to have a ghost. In any case I don't believe in them."

In those early, pre-war days, life at Horton Hall must have been not far short of idyllic for Alfred and Margaret Blunt and the children, Amy, Margaret, David and Geoffrey. The garden was a source of delight particularly to Mrs. Blunt. The older part of the house, which included Abraham's tower with its picturesque circular and lozenge windows, looked out on to a raised rose garden, the beds divided by crazy paving, with an old stone sundial at the centre. On the north side, a great, studded, oak door with a lion's head handle opened on to a neatly paved courtyard adorned with tubs of flowers, and from it an archway led to the drive, lawns and grass tennis court. There was a garage in the yard, and the bishop's chauffeur lived in the cottage which had in former days been occupied by Joshua Smith. The garden had a pretty summerhouse and an old dovecot was brought into use to house three or four dozen white fantail doves.

Inside, the house was very beautiful but difficult to run. A small suite of rooms next to the kitchen was briefly occupied by a cook and a maid, but for most of the time the family relied on daily help. The Blunts lived mainly in the Jacobean part where the bishop's study, which had been Edward Hailstone's library, a fine, panelled dining room and a lovely morning room, also panelled, looked out on to the rose garden. The kitchen, scullery and pantry, dating back to Charles Swaine Booth Sharp's time, were big, high and stone slabbed. Stone steps led up to the level of the Blunts' dining room, and even more to the Georgian part After struggling with this arrangement, Mrs. Blunt had a kitchen made in the Jacobean west wing, next to the Bishop's study and on the same level as their dining room.

From the morning room, a flight of steps led up to the Georgian hall and drawing room - a big, handsome room with an Adam fireplace and plaster work. The family used it occasionally, but it was hard to heat. The other large room on this floor, the great Georgian dining room, was excellent for table tennis when not needed for diocesan meetings. A huge staircase of more than thirty steps rose from the hall. The climb and the problem of heating made the chapel impractical for daily use, but there was a weekly celebration of Holy Communion there. After Amy Blunt's wedding, she and her husband made the other rooms on this floor into a flat for a time.

The rest of the family bedrooms were in the Jacobean part. A staircase led up from the timbered, oak-pillared hall that was the very oldest part of the house to something of a

Bishop Blunt in the Rose Garden

maze of bedrooms and bathrooms, leading off each other and up and down little flights of steps. The magnificent circular, stained glass window, half way up the tower, gave light to the bishop's bathroom. His daughter Margaret's bedroom was Abraham Sharp's study, with its staircase leading to the top of the tower.

Horton Hall was a lovely setting for wedding receptions when Amy was married at All Saints' Church and Margaret at Bradford Cathedral. It was also the venue for sales of work and garden parties in aid of missionary societies, with tables and chairs set out in the courtyard. In 1934, an Anglo-Catholic Congress was held in Bradford Diocese. On its final day, Bishop Blunt led a great procession from All Saints' Church to Horton Hall. A colourful array of vested clergy, choir boys, monks and nuns and many lay people from the parishes of the diocese assembled in the ancient stone-paved courtyard for a service and address by the Archdeacon of York. If there were ghosts, those of the Puritan and Nonconformist Sharps must have been quite surprised, while Royalist John might have hovered above the wall dividing the two halls and permitted himself a sepulchral chuckle.

A newspaper cutting from the Blunt family scrapbook describes the scene :

"Snowy flocks of restless pigeons from the old black and white dovecote wheeled overhead, while hundreds of voices sang a solemn Te Deum. Then guests scattered over green lawns, through pathways lined with hedges of tall, blue and gold and pink lupins, the rhododendron groves and rose gardens, and took tea in the shade of magnificent elms."

In addition to the more formal occasions, Horton Hall was open house to students and clergy. The former Union Workhouse across Little Horton Lane was by this time St. Luke's Hospital, and clergy could easily "drop in" on the Bishop after a hospital visit, and were

Mrs Blunt in the Drawing Room

always welcome. He followed enthusiastically in Bishop Perowne's footsteps in establishing a style far removed from the grandees of former years. It was Bishop Blunt's custom to hold Ordination retreats in his home, with the candidates staying from Thursday until the Ordination Service on Sunday. The teaching to the group and individual interviews were serious and helpful, but mealtimes were relaxed and marked by stories and laughter. It fell to Mrs. Blunt to cater, often unaided, for twenty or so young men, and to be on hand with motherly words of reassurance for the nervous.

Bishop Blunt was the author of many highly acclaimed theological works. A fine definition and exposition of the fundamental principles of Anglican doctrine and worship was first delivered as a Primary Visitation Charge to the clergy of the diocese in 1934, then published by Mowbrays as "C. of E.. What does it stand for?" Two years later, the Bishop sat in his study overlooking the rose garden and thought long and hard about the Presidential Address he was due to give at Bradford Diocesan Conference on December 1st 1936. The subject was to be one which had occupied his mind for some months, namely the forthcoming Coronation of the new King, Edward VIII. He wanted first to counter suggestions that the ceremony should be separated from the sacrament of Holy Communion, and having done this, to consider what he described as "the very much more material point as to the share we can all take in surrounding the Consecration of the King

Interior, oldest part of Horton Hall

with that spiritual atmosphere which is suitable to it."

Out of a finely constructed and reasoned address of some 3000 words, one paragraph leapt from the platform of a small, provincial Diocesan Conference, into the pages of national history. The Bishop said: "In this as in any other sacrament, the benefit which God's grace may effect is dependent upon the presence of certain human conditions. The benefit of the King's Coronation depends under God, upon two elements: Firstly on the faith, prayer and self-dedication of the King himself; and on that it would be improper for me to say anything except to commend him and ask you to commend him to God's grace, which he will so abundantly need, as we all need it - for the King is a man like ourselves - if he is to do his duty faithfully. We hope that he is aware of his need. Some of us wish that he gave more positive signs of such awareness."

A copy of the address was sent, as was customary, to the Yorkshire Post. The Editor, Arthur Mann, who was aware of growing anxiety in high circles about the King's desire to marry Mrs. Simpson, assumed that Bishop Blunt had been authorised to make his comments on a situation that was not general knowledge in the United Kingdom. He based next morning's leading article on the address and sent extracts to the Press Association for circulation. In fact Bishop Blunt had not even heard of Mrs. Simpson when he wrote the address, and although he knew of the situation before delivering it, he had seen no reason to alter his words, which were a reference to the King's general lack of any public

Feeding pigeons in the courtyard.

indication of religious practice or belief.

In retrospect it seems unlikely that the secret could have been kept for much longer, or that a matter of days or weeks would have made the outcome any different. It was Bishop Blunt's misfortune to have been the unwitting key to the opening of the floodgates. Suddenly the Bishop of Bradford was news, not only to the serious media, but to Society and gossip columns. Reporters descended on Horton Hall, looking for photographs and scraps of 'news' about the Bishop and his family. It is unfortunate and unfair that this one incident, not of his making, should have overshadowed an episcopacy of fine achievements and a pattern-setting blend of social and spiritual concern.

1939 brought war again, and for the family at Horton Hall, their share of grief and loss. Both boys joined the armed forces, David in the army, Geoffrey as a pilot officer in the Royal Airforce. In 1941, Geoffrey was killed. He was just nineteen. Only days later, Bishop Blunt wrote an article published in the Sunday Chronicle, "If You Have Lost A Son", which brought comfort and help to many in similar circumstances.

War and its aftermath changed many aspects of the English social scene. Of particular relevance to life at Horton Hall was the changed attitude to domestic service. It had not been easy to find staff for some years, but now it was almost impossible. There had even been some earlier talk of looking for an easier house, but that sort of project was put on hold through the war years. When the war ended, Bishop Blunt was 66 and in poor health

Church Missionary Society Meeting in the courtyard
All photos in this chapter from the Blunt family albums, courtesy of Mr David Blunt

and did not want the upheaval of moving. Hard work though it was, Mrs. Blunt loved the Hall deeply. Her son spoke of her "gathering it round herself" for comfort and security. Visitors became fewer and the surviving children were married and no longer living there. Certainly the Bishop could have retired, perhaps should have retired, but his son David believed that he could not face the prospect of having nothing to do. The matter was decided for him in June 1955. He came home from a Confirmation at Bentham School, the car came up the drive and into the courtyard through the archway, the Bishop looking quite himself, until he got out and wasn't able to walk to the door without help from John Wilkinson, his chauffeur. As he entered the house, he had a severe stroke. He was taken to hospital and returned only briefly to Horton Hall at the end of September, finally retiring and leaving to live his last years in York. Bishop Blunt died in 1957 and was buried in Calverley churchyard beside his son Geoffrey.

The third Bishop of Bradford differed from Bishop Blunt in style and churchmanship. Arthur Perowne and Alfred Blunt had both been modern and progressive in their respective times, but those times had changed, more drastically and rapidly than in any previous era. Donald Coggan brought to Bradford his own modernity, scholarship and enormous drive. In due course he was to become Archbishop of York and then fill the highest office in the Church of England as Archbishop of Canterbury.

Dr. and Mrs. Coggan came to Bradford shortly after the appointment was announced. Lady Powell had died in 1927, aged 94, at her London home, and Horton Hall was rented, now on a yearly lease, from the Powell Estates. The house the Coggans were shown round in 1955 was gloomy and uninviting. Margaret Pawley describes it in her biography, "Donald Coggan, Servant of Christ":

"The house represented a hotch-potch of architectural styles; it was pretentious, rambling, cold and difficult to maintain; the kitchen had equipment that called for the application of black-lead, and the garden was large and neglected."

Gone were the days of gleaming polished oak, of sunlight streaming into a study from a lovingly tended rose garden. The days of wheeling white doves, tennis parties and young people's laughter could never return. Even longer gone were the dinners and soirees when the cream of local society gathered in the gracious Georgian rooms. The great days of Abraham Sharp's industry and genius were all but forgotten, and only abandoned outbuildings spoke of the bustle of a self supporting farmstead in a pre-industrial age. It was little wonder that the new Bishop and his family felt it was not for them, particularly as Bradford was the only diocese with such an arrangement of a rented house. For the diocese, the time had come to finally give up what had, thirty five years ago, been intended as a temporary arrangement.

A modern See house was bought in Heaton, smaller than Horton Hall, infinitely more convenient to run and a source of delight to Mrs. Coggan and their two daughters as their first settled home. *(Margaret Pawley's biography describes the unsatisfactory domestic arrangements which went with some of Donald Coggan's earlier academic posts.)*

Ruth Hook, wife of the fifth Bishop of Bradford, who came in 1972, deeply regretted the severing of the diocesan connection with the hall. She said she would have a thousand times preferred the historic house, however inconvenient and would have gladly taken it on. The present See house she described as superb for its purpose, easy to run, in every way a good bishop's house, but for all that, a vulgar house.

The Sharps built Horton Hall, enlarged it, improved it and made it an estate of real significance in the locality. In their generations they served God and their country fearlessly, according to their consciences. Their scholarship and skill made real contributions to both theological and scientific development.

Many of those who subsequently occupied their home made their own significant contributions, almost as if the spirit of the place had entered into them. Alfred Blunt, scholar, social reformer and faithful servant of his God, left Horton Hall in October 1955 and nobody ever lived there again.

Horton Hall and Garden in 1938
Horton Old Hall can just be seen, bottom left, and the spire of All Saints' church immediately below Horton Hall. the large new building is the Nurses' Home and St Luke's Hospital is on the right of Little Horton Lane, on land which was once part of Horton Hall estate.   (print supplied courtesy of Woods Visual Imaging Ltd)

Chapter 13
Epilogue

Horton Hall stood empty, an anachronism, a run-down country estate surrounded by town. Horton Old Hall, smaller and possibly more immediately appealing for twentieth century use, had fared no better. It had not been lived in since before the Second World War. Lady Powell died in 1927 at her London home, and shortly after, the contents of Horton Old Hall were removed. Among them, what looked like a bundle of dirty, wet rags in an outbuilding was seen to be a tapestry, and taken to Cartwright Hall for cleaning. A year or two later, antiques from Horton Old Hall were sold at Sotheby's, including the tapestry which depicted Biblical scenes and had been made in the Low Countries in 1550. It sold for 3,200 guineas.

During the war, the Old Hall was used by the Army. They looked after the building and left it in good condition, but it was almost impossible to prevent a certain amount of damage to large, unoccupied houses standing in extensive grounds. The two halls proved irresistible adventure playgrounds for local youth, and both suffered accidental damage as well as some outright vandalism, after which the weather also took its toll.

Leeds Regional Hospital Board was interested in the sites of both halls in connection with plans to redevelop St. Luke's Hospital, and their proposals were put to Bradford Council's Public Works Committee in 1959. In September of that year, the Committee approved the proposal of the Hospital Board to use Horton Hall and Horton Old Hall for hospital purposes, subject to the buildings not being demolished. Only two months later, that position had shifted to require only that the 17th century portion of Horton Hall be retained and the internal panelling of Horton Old Hall be preserved.

The halls were bought by the Hospital Board from the Sharp-Powell Estate in 1960. Planning permission to demolish Horton Old Hall had been granted, and although Horton Hall was a Grade I listed building, the Ministry of Housing and Local Government in Harold MacMillan's Government lifted the preservation order, after initial refusals.

Horton Hall stood directly in the line of probable development and Bradford City Council now gave its permission. The minutes of the Town Planning and Building Committee, approved by the Public Works Committee, dated 3rd July 1963, read:

"the view of this Sub-Committee that the 17th century portion of Horton Hall be retained and the internal panelling of Horton Old Hall be preserved, be withdrawn, and that the decision of the Sub-Committee of 11th November 1959 and 15th November1961, and the resolution passed by the Sub-Committee 1st May 1963 relative to these matters be rescinded."

In August, Mr. W. Bowring, Secretary of Leeds Regional Hospital Board, announced that both halls were to be demolished because of the high cost of restoring them.

Bradford Civic Society and Peter Bird, Director of the City Art Gallery, battled to save what could be saved. They emphasised the history and significance of the halls and in September 1963 the Civic Society delivered a petition with more than 17 pages of signatures and many other letters, urging the Council to secure the preservation of Horton Old Hall as a museum or some other purpose for the benefit of the citizens of Bradford. There were letters from concerned individuals and organisations in the local newspapers.

Some of the lost plasterwork

The Bradford Historical and Antiquarian Society appealed for the saving of Horton Hall, and local historian and writer Wade Hustwick wrote articles reminding Bradfordians of the history and importance of the halls. Even after the Council's capitulation in July 1963, Richard Harrison, the Keeper of Bolling Hall Museum, wrote to the Yorkshire Post with a plea to save both buildings. Horton Hall, he said, was one of the finest pieces of domestic architecture of the 17th century in the Bradford area, despite the fact that one wing had been replaced by a structure completely out of proportion to the rest. It was also one of the very few dated smaller buildings with a known designer.

Peter Bird and the Art Galleries Committee suggested Horton Old Hall, which was in a better state of repair, could house the schools museum service, craft workshops, and a collection of 19th century vehicles in the outbuildings. There were talks with the Director of Education about using it as a combined Schools Service Department, children's museum, picture loan centre and general extra-mural department of the City Art Galleries and Museums. Demolition of the Old Hall was not essential to the Hospital Board's plans, and they were willing to negotiate a sale to Bradford Council, but in 1966 the Finance Policy Advisory Sub-Committee recommended that no action be taken, and that building's fate was sealed.

Because of its position in relation to Hospital Board plans, there was no hope of saving Horton Hall, once permission to demolish the listed building had been given. The best that could be hoped for was the preservation of some of its features. Richard Harrison put the case for one of the most important:

"Horton Hall Porch Tower - built in early 1670, extended upwards by Abraham Sharp about 1700 and used as an observatory. As such, it is the only monument, apart from the Royal Greenwich Observatory, illustrating the advancement of English science during the 17th century, certainly the only observatory tower in the provinces. Architecturally it contains two windows of considerable importance. The lower wheel window is one of the largest of its kind and the latest dated example in the West Riding. The lozenge shaped

Hanover Gardens on the site of Horton Old Hall. (photo: J. Hansen)

The Author at the site of Horton Hall. (photo: J. Hansen)

window above it is unique."

Eventually the front face of the tower was carefully taken down, its stones numbered and their positions recorded on a plan, but even then, the City Engineer could find nowhere to store them, and the demolition contractors had to ask repeatedly for them to be removed from the site. They are now in the custody of the Museums Department, but no suitable site for their re-erection and display has yet been found.

Other treasures were even less fortunate. Sir Francis Sharp-Powell's heirs, the Bardsley-Powell family, asked for an Adam fireplace, a 17th century fireplace and the weathercock. Apart from these items, a list was drawn up of items to be considered for removal - mullioned windows, carved Tudor fireplaces, Italian mosaic panels and plaster ceilings and friezes. In January 1965, under the expert supervision of a technician from the Art Galleries and Museums department, workmen began the careful removal of Revd. Thomas Sharp's fine 17th century plaster ceilings. The ceilings were cut free and carefully lowered into trays of sawdust. Two were safely down, and left on the floor, with one more to be cut down next day, before all were to be taken to one of the museums. During that night, a night watchman at the nearby Nurses' Home saw a red glow in the building and raised the alarm. By the time the fire brigade arrived, the basement, ground and first floors were well alight, flames fanning out of the observatory tower. Ancient oak panelling burned fiercely, floors collapsed, and the trays of plasterwork crashed through into the basement. In a statement to the Telegraph and Argus, Peter Bird said that the last ceiling, with centre rose and the Sharp arms appeared to be intact, and work would continue to remove and preserve this important artefact. The Bradford Museums department has no record of it ever having reached them, so it would seem that the attempt failed.

Horton Hall and Horton Old Hall vanished as though they had never been. And for what? No hospital building appeared on the site of either. In the 1980s Hanover Gardens, a development of flats for elderly people, was built on the site of Horton Old Hall, designed so that its shape is reminiscent of the house that once stood there. The old wall that separated a family divided by civil war still stands, serving now to seclude the pleasant and peaceful housing development from the tarmacadam expanse of a car park for hospital visitors which obliterates every last trace of Horton Hall and its gardens.

Bibliography

Chapman Allan	Dividing the Circle	John Wiley & Sons in association with Praxis Publishing 1995
Cudworth William	Life and Correspondence of Abraham Sharp	Thos. Brear & Co. 1889
Cudworth William	Rambles Round Horton	Thos. Brear & Co. 1886
Fieldhouse Joseph	Bradford	Watmoughs Ltd. & Bradford Metropolitan Council Libraries 1987
Hansen Astrid	One Small Corner	Bradford Diocesan Board of Finance 1994
Hart A. Tindal	The Life and Times of John Sharp Archbishop of York	SPCK 1949
Holroyd Abraham	Collectanea Bradfordiana	1873
Hulbert H.L.P.	Sir Francis Sharp Powell, Baronet and Member of Parliament	1914
James John	The History and Topography of Bradford	1841
King Henry C	The History of the Telescope	Griffin 1955
Richardson Clement	A Geography of Bradford	University of Bradford 1977
Scruton William	Pen and Pencil Pictures of Old Bradford	1890
Selby C.W.	The Hailstone Papers 1696 - 1871	

Bradford Textile Society Journals

Bradford Portraits of Influential Citizens   ed. J.R.Beckett 1892

Index

Illustrations in Bold

Act of Uniformity	27
All Saints' Church	60, 63, **64, 65**, 68, 75
Balme, Matthew	48
Bamburgh	44
Blunt, Alfred, Bishop	72, 74ff, **75**
Blunt, Amy	74, 75
Blunt, David	74, 78
Blunt, Geoffrey	74, 78, 79
Blunt, Margaret	74, 75
Blunt, Mrs Margaret	74, **76**, 79
Bolling Hall	9, 20, 83
Booth, Charles Swaine	43ff
Bradford Cathedral	72
Bradford Church Building Society	63
Bradford Civic Society	82
Bradford Diocese	68
Bradford Festival Choral Society	58
Bradford Grammar School	25, 26, 30, 56, 67
Bradford Parish Church	15, 19, 39, 42, 51 60, 68
Bradford Workhouse	54, 75
Bridges, Francis Sharp	61
Bull, Revd. Geo. Stringer	47, 48
Cawthra, Joseph	**66,** 67
Ceulen, Ludolph van	40
Civil War	15, 18ff
Clarkson, David	17, **19**, 20, 25
Clarkson, Mary (Sharp)	16, 20, 25
Clarkson, Robert	16, 19, 32
Clarkson, William	16, 19, 27
Coggan, Donald, Bishop	79
Craven, Archdeacon of	56
Croft House	50, 52, 61
Dawson, Revd. Eli	39
Edward VIII, King	76
Fairfax, Ferdinando, Lord	18
Fairfax, Thomas, Sir	18, **20**, 21
Family Trees	12, 13, 14
Fayre Gappe	16
Ferrand, Sarah Harriette Lilla	59
Ferrand, William Busfeild	59
Flamsteed, John	**31**, 32ff, 42
Giles, Ann	45, 46, 53, 54, 61
Giles, Edmund	45, 61
Gilpin, Hannah	43, 45
Gilpin, Thomas	45
Graham, George	33
Great Exhibition	58
Greenwich National Maritime Museum	37
Greenwich Royal Observatory	32, 37, 83
Hailstone, Ann	51
Hailstone, Edward	51ff, 54ff, **55, 59**, 65
Hailstone, Jane	56
Hailstone, John	51ff, 56
Hailstone, Samuel	50ff, 61
Halley, Edmund	33, 34, 40
Hammond, Ezra Waugh	**66**
Hanover Gardens	**84**, 85
Hardy, Annis	48
Hardy, John	48, 50
Harrison, John	41
Heywood, Revd. Oliver	39
Historia Coelestis Britannica	33
Horton Chapel	39, 41
Horton Hall Illustrations	**28, 43, 44, 75, 76, 77, 78, 79, 81, 83, 84**
Plans	**24, 57, 62**
Horton House, Rugby	51
Horton Old Hall	18, 22, **29**, 39, 60, 63, 82, 83
Kirkstall	9, 15
Lacy, Richard	16
Leeds Regional Hospital Board	82
Leventhorpe, William de	9
Lister, Joseph	20
London Science Museum	37
Longitude	40
Mill Hill Chapel	27
Mixenden Chapel	39
Moon, features named after Abraham Sharp	42
Morley Independent Chapel	27
Mossman, Frederick A.T.	68
Mossman, George	50, 68
Mural Arc	**32**, 33
Newcastle, Earl of	9, 20
Newton, Sir Isaac	26, 33, 42
Oastler, Richard	46, **47**
Over Hall, Shipley	25
Perowne, Arthur, Bishop	69ff, **70**, 79
Perowne, Helena	69, 71
Perowne, Leslie	71
Perowne, Stewart	71
Powell, Annie	61, 68, 79

Powell, Francis Sharp	61ff, **63**
Priestley, Revd. Nathaniel	39
Ramsden, Jesse	38
Rand, John	46
Rawson, William	23
Ripon, Bishop of	48, 56, 59, 68, 69
Royds Hall	10
Rugby School	52
Sadler, Michael	47
St. Catherine's House	67
St. George's Hall	56, **58**
St. James' Church	48, **49**
St. Luke's Hospital	75, 82
Sawrey, Faith	43, 66
Sawrey, Richard	41
Sharp – note: not all members of the Sharp family are indexed	
Sharp, Abraham	9, 22, 30ff, **30, 37**, 43, 65, 80, 83
Calculations	**34**
Mural Arc	**32**
Telescope	**36**
Sharp, Catharine	44
Sharp, Faith	27, 29, 34, 41
Sharp, Lieutenant Isaac	18, 22, 39
Sharp, Isaac	61
Sharp, John, Archbishop	15, 26, 44
Sharp, John, Dr.	29, 35, 38
Sharp, John, Parliamentarian	18ff, 22
Sharp, John, Royalist	16
Sharp, Thomas, Clothier	15, 51
Sharp, Revd. Thomas	22ff, 34, 85
Sharp, William	**51**, 51ff
Shipley Hall	23
Smeaton, John	37
Smith, Alderman S	58
Smith, Revd. Matthew	39
Squaring the Circle	39
Stansfield, Elizabeth and Robert	41
Stansfield, Faith	41
Stapleton, Dorothy	42, 61
Ten Hours Bill	48
Towne End, Leeds	29
Waterhouse, Richard & Susan	16
Whitaker, Dr. T.D.	9, 52
White, Mr & Mrs Albert Norman	67, 68
White, Norman Arthur	67
Wibsey Chapel	27
Wood, John	**46**, 46ff, 52
Wood, Thomas	16
Worcester, Bishop of	72
Wright, Matthew	66
York, Archbishop Musgrave of	56
York Museums	37, 58